IN THEIR
OWN WORDS

BRUCE POLLOCK

Collier Books

A Division of Macmillan Publishing Co., Inc.

New York

Collier Macmillan Publishers

London

Macmillan Publishing Co., Inc.
866 Third Avenue, New York, N.Y. 10022
Collier-Macmillan Canada Ltd.

Library of Congress Cataloging in Publication Data

Pollock, Bruce.
   In their own words.

   1. Rock musicians.   2. Music, Popular
(Songs, etc.)
—Writing and publishing.   I.   Title.
[ML3561.R62P64   1975b]   784   75–1387

In Their Own Words is available in a hardcover
edition by Macmillan Publishing Co., Inc.

"HOMETEAM CROWD" by Loudon Wainwright III.
© 1972 FRANK MUSIC CORP. Used by permission.

The photograph of Doc Pomus is by Damon
Runyon, Jr. The photograph of Gerry Goffin is
by Barbara Goffin.

Collier Books Edition 1975

Printed in the United States of America

This book is dedicated to:
"Mom, The Gang, and My Baby"

CONTENTS

INTRODUCTION: 1974

In 1973 when the adolescent form turned eighteen, even cynics had to admit that rock 'n' roll had truly come of age. It had outlived the expectations of its staunchest critics, had in fact grown fat where other styles had faltered, had become a way of life for its adherents. Old enough to be legally married in most states, to die on the battlefield for its country, to be given the vote at last, rock 'n' roll clearly deserved the full respect of its elders—pop, jazz, blues, and the classics.

A product of the war-baby generation, rock 'n' roll appealed mostly to white middle-class kids from good neighborhoods and the suburbs. Combining urban black music with the country and western mournfulness of the backwoods hillbilly, it gave universal voice to the concerns of the new adolescent class. An extraordinarily verbal generation, they took their music out of high school and into the changing world of civil rights, sexual freedom, dope, the draft, and revolution to create a living myth for the audience, the future writers, and the performers.

First came consciousness along the fringe, isolated action; then came Bob Dylan and Phil Ochs and the protest movement. Then "Blowin' in the Wind" made the Top Ten charts. Rock 'n' roll and the course of events in a circle of cause and effect.

This and succeeding generations can write their autobiographies in terms of rock 'n' roll. "Everybody," by Tommy Roe, was playing on the radio when the first bulletin of President Kennedy's assassination reached me. "Calcutta," by Lawrence

Welk, was the tune I watched myself dancing to on a delayed videotape of the "Bob Crewe Generation" swinging teen dance show. I was in San Francisco the weekend after Bobby Kennedy was shot, among hundreds of milling hippies at Golden Gate Park where a free concert previously scheduled by the Grateful Dead and the Jefferson Airplane was cancelled in deference to the event.

During the sixties many lived a self-imposed poverty; poets were created and songwriters, who arose, scruffy, from each neighborhood became millionaires. Spurred on by the music and the lyrics, the generation got so high watching itself rise to power (on the Cult of Youth wave), toppling universities and presidents (often university presidents), that it became arrogant and deluded, tried to take on the law itself, and ultimately fell under the guns of Washington.

In the seventies there is balm for the wounds. An era is over. Easy listening love songs and nostalgia for the fifties, the forties, and the thirties promote a noncommitted time.

But rock 'n' roll still lives. It did not die with the fervor of the sixties; it merely put on false eyelashes, a dress, and high heels and assumed majority flexing its muscles, full of the snide confidence necessary to take on the adult world (now that the acne had healed).

Far from being a fad, the music itself is a spawning ground for myriad trends to unwind upon, growing larger with each absorbed style. It has, in fact, gone on to become the biggest kid on the block, carrying more pure bulk than either of its famous next-door neighbors, T.V. and Film.

For the young people of today the popular song, especially as presented in albums, is the quickest and most satisfying method of expression. In an era where all other forms of artistic endeavor are highly limited and restrictive, only the field of songwriting is relatively open to the young creative artist. New works by the songwriters are anticipated with the same eagerness prior generations bestowed on their novelists, poets, and playwrights. And criticized with the same seriousness of purpose, to be placed in rank alongside other worthy efforts of the era. Already we have our rock scholars and historians, our sociologists and philosophers.

The music as it stands before us today owes as much of a debt to Hank Williams as it does to Cole Porter and goes back in a straight line to Robert Johnson and Woody Guthrie. Schooled on that literature the new writers came up, each adding their own defining touch: Chuck Berry giving it a name, Bob Dylan reshaping it with anguish and absurdity, Phil Ochs adding a social conscience, John Sebastian providing high style and grace.

As a member of the original rock 'n' roll generation and an addict for nearly two decades, I find objectivity impossible. In my youth I fell hard for "Jo-ann," "Diana," and "Peggy Sue," and none of these new chicks give me the same thrill. Reluctantly I bid farewell to those good girls to spend the night with "Suzanne," the morning after with "Ruby Tuesday."

So it goes. This book is history, autobiography, textbook, oral report, song of praise. It is writers on writing. Rock 'n' roll stars on rock 'n' roll. Former listeners to Elvis and Dylan becoming idols themselves. Inside there are lyricists, singer/songwriters, artists, and craftsmen. Those whose words form the current lyrical spectrum from pop to folk to rock to show music.

HAL DAVID

Most people think of Hal David solely as the silent, lyric-writing partner in the musical team of Bacharach and David, and in terms of the multitude of pop-classics born of that union.

However, he has worked with many other composers and has written songs for such varied performers as Dionne Warwick, Frank Sinatra, Sarah Vaughn, and Elvis Presley.

Already well into his career at the time of the rock 'n' roll takeover, Hal David offers a unique perspective of a writer able to coexist in any number of styles without having to change his basic lyrical approach, and has thus served as both a continuation of a breed of writers schooled in pop and show tunes (including his oldest brother, Mack David) and a model for a younger generation of romantic songwriters, typified by someone like Paul Williams.

The interview with Hal David took place at City Center, in Manhattan.

"I loved rock 'n' roll. I used to listen to other writers who were very establishment oriented—as if there were such a thing as an establishment—who would hate rock 'n' roll and thought it was a fad. I never could understand that kind of thinking. It's part of the environment; it's part of young people. I have two sons and I saw it happening before it necessarily became a big thing. I remember the first time I heard Elvis Presley. He recorded a number of songs for a company called Sun Records, down South, before RCA Victor went and paid him a fortune. I happened to hear him because one of the songs was a song my brother wrote, called 'I Don't Care If The Sun Don't Shine.' So I heard that whole thing, and I tell you, it was sensational. Eventually I wrote a few songs for a movie he was in. I can't remember the name of the movie; I didn't see it, but I loved having him sing the songs.

"I keep up with today's music in my own way. I listen to the radio. I hear all the records of the people my son likes. We start off with that premise, and I'm conditioned somewhat by his taste. I like or don't like what I hear on his record machine.

"Song lyrics are more varied than they were in the twenties

and thirties and the forties, which I think is terrific. They deal with all sorts of subjects that were not acceptable on the radio at one time. Everybody is going further and further in what is acceptable in a public place . . . and radio is a public place.

"For example, I wrote a song called 'The Windows Of The World,' which deals with war and is one of my favorite songs. Chances are if I wrote that song around World War Two, which would be my war, or World War One, which would be somebody else's war, it certainly would not have been acceptable on the radio. I probably never would have thought of it, because I would have been conditioned another way, conditioned that you're saving the world for something, or someone —which proved to be not necessarily very true. The feeling that war doesn't save anybody, it just kills people, is very valid today. I think the times permit you to say certain things.

"But I don't think in terms of whether a song is commercial or not. I mean, I have opinions, but I don't let them guide me in terms of what songs I'm going to write. I know enough to know I don't know what will be a hit until it becomes a hit . . . and I suspect very few people do know, if anybody does. But I think I know a good song from a song that's not good. So I try to write good songs instead of hit songs."

We talked about specific work habits, the problems involved with collaboration.

"It's a two way situation—the melody has to feel like it was made for the lyric and the lyric like it was made for the melody, and to do that requires an accommodation of sorts. It shouldn't look like there's an accommodation. One should just mesh into the other. If you're able to tell which was written first, the lyric or the melody, there's something wrong with the song. I mean, every once in a while I'll play that game too and sometimes I'm right, but I would never ask the question unless there was something in the song that bothered me. When you write to a melody you're trying to find what the melody is saying, just as the composer is trying to find what the lyric is saying. That may seem easier because it's language as opposed to something as abstract as music, but every piece of music says something.

"Sometimes I write against the music, but I hear things that way too. In other words, when I hear 'Do You Know The Way To San Jose?' or 'Raindrops Keep Fallin' On My Head,' the music is gay and bright and rhythmic and because of that it's instinctively happy to a lot of people. It isn't always instinctively happy to me.

"Working with a collaborator you must also learn to be politic. I don't know if that's the right word, but if you have something to say about his melody, you have to find a nice way of saying it. I mean, you can't go around saying you like things if you don't like them, at least I think you're crazy if you do. And so, first of all, you don't react immediately if you don't like something. You say, 'I'd like to hear it again.' There are many ways you can do it. You say, 'Well, I don't know . . .'

"The most difficult thing to establish for yourself once you become a successful songwriter, is to find honest criticism, because people assume you know more than they do, and they tend to like things that they might not like if somebody else wrote them. So somewhere in your mind you have to develop— I'm not crazy about the word humility, but that's the word— you have to develop a sense of humility about yourself, so you're not on a real ego trip. So when everybody is telling you how good it is, how great it is, you know that maybe it is, maybe it isn't . . . but they're saying it, firstly, because they're trying to be kind and generous. So you start with that. Then you have to go to your collaborator, who is a sounding board for you, as you're a sounding board for him—and that's important.

"Probably the most important critics for me are my wife and both my sons. Just on the basis of how they say they like a song. I've been married a long time and I really know my wife and her reactions, and just the way she says something tells me how she feels.

"So, when I work with a collaborator, I work two ways, by myself and with the collaborator. Every night I'd work on some new ideas or try to finish something we worked on that afternoon. When you're in rehearsals for a show, it entails more than writing; it entails working with the singers, meetings about the sound. You stay with a play, all of a sudden it's a whole family.

"If I'm working in the city I'll start at ten, ten-thirty. Mostly I like to work at home. It's easier. I have an office in the back where I have everything I need. I sort of walk around the house —I don't lock myself in the office. I work with a pencil and a yellow legal pad. I only type when I'm all finished.

"I try to write in the morning if I'm home, by eight-thirty or nine. I'll have coffee and grapefruit; then I go into my office. Of course I try to avoid getting down to it—I'll start making phone calls or hope that somebody calls me. To me the beginning of work is always the toughest. I don't mean the beginning of every day; I mean the beginning of starting on a project. Say I have to write a song for a show, or do four new songs for an album, or whatever it is I'm doing. I tend not to write *a* song anymore—I don't know why but I just don't. So just to get myself revved up is the most difficult part, but once I get myself up it's okay. It's harder now than at first to get to the point where I'm saying, 'Hey, I gotta do this,' but easier to write once I'm started.

"For instance, next week there's a little project I really want to do, so I'm going to try to attack that. It's a question of four songs. Usually I have a number of things and of those things one of them is where I want to be next. This project I'll work on till it's done because it's something very offbeat and interesting. Then hopefully there'll be a show or an interesting album . . . there are a few things I'm sort of in the talking stages about, or thinking about.

"Those things almost present themselves at the right time

as that's the next one you're going to do. Everything falls into place, that's the one you like, that has the least problems and the timing is right for everyone involved."

I asked him if he'd ever gone through any extended periods when he was not writing.

"I don't know how extended they are, but I do go through periods of not writing, which I never did prior to now, but it's out of choice. When I've had blocks in the past it's been a case of I'm not getting what I want. My blocks tend to be that everything's a little tougher for me. I don't have literal blocks where all of a sudden it just doesn't come. Sometimes I just struggle with a song a little bit longer."

Not having a hit on the charts is another matter.

"I remember one particular time when I wasn't having much success. I think generally when you go through a bad period you panic a little bit the first time and you think, 'Oh my God, it's all over!' And then you start moving again. The next time it happens you react a little less. Finally you just take it for granted it's going to happen from time to time.

"This particular time, not the first time, I was sitting at breakfast with my wife and sons. I always had breakfast with them as they were going off to school. And the radio was on, as always, and I didn't have any hits going or anything exciting happening, and my older son, Jimmy, said—just after a big hit song had played—he said, 'You know Dad, you ought to write songs like that and maybe you'd have some hits.' You know he didn't mean to be unkind, but he sure was! That kind of really socked me, and I didn't find it amusing at the time. There's nothing sweeter than a hit."

We discussed Hal David's beginnings as a songwriter, a career which started taking shape as far back as his early childhood.

"I had sort of, not a unique childhood as far as songwriters are concerned, because there's been a few others like me, but it's fairly unique. I have a brother who's a successful songwriter, and when I was a boy we used to sit around the radio. That was the day of the big bands, and during that time the publishers knew when their songs were being performed. You know, Guy Lombardo was playing your song at twelve o'clock at the Roosevelt Hotel or Tommy Dorsey was playing it at this particular time or Dennis Day was going to do it on the Jack Benny show. So you knew ahead of time, and we used to stay up to all hours of the morning to hear my brother's songs, which were some very big ones—'Just A Kid Named Joe,' 'Johnny Zero.' He had some other very big hits—'Candy,' 'I Don't Care If The Sun Don't Shine,' 'Cherry Pink,' 'La Vie En Rose'—but they were further on. I was older.

"In some ways his success was an intimidating thing to me, but I thought I was pretty good. I showed him my songs and he was very encouraging, but he didn't encourage me to become a songwriter. He thought I'd be smarter getting into advertising, that's where the big money is. I studied journalism and I worked for the *New York Post* a long, long time ago . . . and he approved of that kind of a thing. Songwriting he didn't think was quite so legitimate for his kid brother."

I asked Hal for his opinion on the difference between a professional lyric and one turned out by an amateur, one of the millions who daily take up songwriting for fun and profit, for ego-gratification and party spotlights.

"The big difference, I guess, between an amateur and a professional—and that has nothing to do necessarily with talent and lack of talent—is experience. I try not to think in terms of amateur and professional. I've seen some things done by amateurs that are rough and without the polish that I, for example, try for in a lyric—but that's the way I write. The roughness very often, the rub of it, is something that attracks me. In other words an amateur, the quality of his work may be rougher and the professional's, a lot smoother . . . but bad smooth is not as good as good rough. I would rather think in terms of good and bad, because a professional has just spent more time at it . . . and time doesn't make you wiser, it just makes you older.

"In other words, as a lyric writer, speaking from what I know, I hope I *see* more today than I did twenty-five years ago. I hope my ears are attuned to hearing more. When I hear a phrase, hopefully I can hear all around that phrase and in that phrase, so my thinking is not as limited. My view, if I'm walking someplace, especially if my mind is working, is hopefully like that of an artist, who will walk down the street and see things. A painter will see things that I won't see because his vision has expanded. And hopefully as an artist—and I like to think I am—I will see more than someone who is not a writer. I should.

"The form of songwriting is a very restrictive form because it's in a very small frame. It's not free like prose could be, like a play or a novel or even free verse poetry. But because of its restrictions you get a bonus you couldn't get in any other form. Because it's in this little microcosm, if it works it should just burst out of there; it should have a greater explosion, a greater impact. And I think that's why songs perhaps have a greater impact on the public than almost any other form of creative work.

"I don't think it's just because it's a popular art form, which it is—the young people grow up living it and understanding it, so it's second nature to them, like their language—but also it has that tremendous impact when it works. It doesn't take so long to get there. It's not two hours until it's fulfilled; or a novel that will take you a few nights to read.

"The only thing like it is probably painting or sculpture. For one who understands the medium, nothing works faster. But unfortunately not as many people understand, are as well versed in the painting and sculpture world as they are in music. You grow up with music. Somewhere along the way you get blocked with painting. I think I'm unblocked now with painting, but for years everything stopped for me with the Impressionist period. I'd go to museums with my wife, who's an artist, but

I never really understood it. But by looking and talking and meeting artists, I finally began to break through. And now it's wonderful for me.

"But, summing up, I suspect nobody quite knows what they're listening for in a song. I was always drawn to lyrics, but I was conscious of music as well. I played violin. It was a form of Jewish culture; everybody played violin in my family . . . and I loved music and we always had music at home. But my whole drive, my whole thrust has always been words. All the way through school my interest was in writing short stories, writing poems, writing for the school paper and the school magazine. I finally put that writing to use in a book of my lyrics that was published. I had notes along with the lyrics, different comments that were appropriate."

I asked him how he thought his lyrics looked on the printed page.

"I think if they're good lyrics they should be quite readable and enjoyable. They look terrific!"

PART
ONE

Growing Pains:
1955–1962

(Indoctrination

Stage)

"Rock Around The Clock," by Freedman and DeKnight, 1955

Nineteen fifty-five. In the beginning there was rhythm and blues. Bobby Zimmerman was still recovering from his bar mitzvah in Minnesota. John Lennon and Paul McCartney had short hair in the slums of Liverpool. Elvis Presley drove a truck in Mississippi. Donny Osmond had not even been born. In the upper wavelengths of American radio Dick Clark and Allen Freed were changing the course of history in soundless chambers of the night. For the first time middle-class white kids, in cities everywhere, began picking up on black music, in the midnight hour after their parents were asleep.

Rock 'n' roll's first classic, "Rock Around The Clock," written by a couple of post-fifty-year-old Tin Pan Alley veterans, appeared in the movie *Blackboard Jungle*—which was about street punks, hoods, and greasers. Black music moving one step closer to home. For the average white middle-class war-baby city kid, going on ten perhaps, the black experience was remote and inspired fear. Hoods were more prevalent in the neighborhood. They were older, sixteen at least, and seemed to represent all the horrible changes puberty was supposed to bring about. They smoked cigarettes, slicked their hair back with Max Factor's Crewcut, and hung around pizza parlors guzzling brew and dancing to Chuck Berry R&B records on the jukebox. A day's recreation for a hood was to play "salugee" with your brand-new Brooklyn Dodgers baseball cap. The black experience, rhythm and blues, *Blackboard Jungle*, hoods—these were the auspicious beginnings of rock 'n' roll.

"Hound Dog," by Leiber and Stoller, 1956

Elvis Presley on "The Ed Sullivan Show"; a hood made good, hillbilly greaser with sex appeal, singing the black experience with country-boy primitive delight, rocking his hips, rolling his eyes, driving teen-age girls and their parents each a different kind of crazy. The following Monday in high schools and junior high schools all across the country, Elvis types sprang up, hoods and would-be hoods, hicks and aspiring hicks, wearing their pants three sizes too small in the crotch, taps on their shoes, hair dripping grease.

For thoses old-fashioned souls who still dressed like Perry Como in a comfortable sweater or Bing Crosby in a cockeyed fedora and for those who sometimes crooned in front of the bedroom mirror songs like "Racing With The Moon" and "I'll Never See Maggie Alone," the change was nearly devastating. Suddenly all the girls were swooning over Elvis and Elvis look-alikes—even that special one, third row first seat, whom you'd been secretly in love with the last six weeks. So it became imperative to shed the sweater and hat for tight sexy pants, to trade in the Keds for Italian pointy-toe dancing shoes, to incorporate a Southern drawl into sophisticated recess conversation.

Of course, some could not manage this and were left in the dust. Others sadly said goodbye to Bill Hayes and "The Ballad Of Davy Crockett" and hello to "Hound Dog."

"Diana," by Paul Anka, 1957

By 1957 rock 'n' roll's first great wave had broken. Two years of being alternately entranced and terrified by the rhythm and blues-based country-soul rocking of Elvis and his fellow greasers imitating imaginary blacks had done its magic. Kids finally gave up the secure world of Perry and Bing and advanced into the unknown of rock 'n' roll—one part the pop music of adults, one part the rhythm and blues of the blacks and the imitative greasers, and one part their own special something.

(There are those today who refer to the rhythm and blues period of rock as the first and last hurrah for this music, which they feel has gone steadily downhill since then into commercialism, updated pop, and pseudo-intellectual gibberish. These R&B freaks, with their stacks of precious, rare 45s on labels long since out of print and their obscure magazines about obscure groups no longer working, live imprisoned in 1956. They can still be seen haunting the same candy store where they grew up, even though they are now thirty-five and the neighborhood has changed. Nothing can be said to convince these people they have not been betrayed. And they are not the only generation to have that feeling about their mother music.)

The rest of the rabble feasted on the images, grew fat on the knowledge of how others saw them and how they saw themselves. The music was simple, direct, easy to listen to, easy to play. You did not have to hire a hall to make this music, nor a band for accompaniment. All you needed was a song. In Coney Island at the time there was a place where you could make demonstration discs for fifty cents apiece—yourself on vocal, your next door neighbor playing three chords on guitar. This demo could then be sent in an unmarked brown envelope to that girl in the third row. Your song might be entitled "Joann," or "Kathy-O," or even "Diana." If your heart was pure it would be rock 'n' roll.

Paul Anka was the generation's first rock 'n' roll prodigy. At thirteen he could play, he could write, he could sing—a three letter man. It is said that Anka wrote "Diana," for his sixteen-year-old baby-sitter on whom he had a crush. Even if thirteen *is* pretty old to have a baby-sitter, Anka's lyric ("I'm so young and you're so old . . .") still defined one of the central problems of adolescence: Girls grow up faster than boys.

It was one of the grimmer facts of life that at thirteen most girls were taller, heavier, stronger, brighter, faster, and generally more imposing than any boy below the age of fifteen . . . and would remain so for two or three more agonizing years. The average thirteen-year-old male hung around the local public-school playground scouting incoming fifth-grade girls. Girls his own age, meanwhile, were being asked out by high-school boys, who shaved nearly twice a week! To date a girl of the same age in junior high school, one had to be incredibly sharp, filthy rich, or built like a pro tackle. Imagine the sheer nerve of a fellow like Anka then, rather short, who set his sights on a girl three years his senior! Such is the power of rock 'n' roll.

"Chances Are," by Stillman and Allen, 1957

Sex was no casual thing in 1957. Thirteen-year-old girls were still virgins and intended to remain that way. Boys were just as inexperienced. The best you could hope for was a little heavy necking in your family's finished basement after a Saturday-night date. Still, that first move was always a moment filled with terror, as boy and girl sat leg to leg on the couch in the darkness.

No one could aid a fumbling lover better than Johnny Mathis. Put the most calculated mush into his mouth and it came out poetry. A little taste of Johnny on the old Victrola and heaven could be had for nearly three minutes. Or if you'd been really clever and purchased a Johnny Mathis *album* (two weeks' allowance) perhaps seventeen minutes of uninterrupted bliss were in the offing—"It's Not For Me To Say," "Wonderful, Wonderful," "Misty,"—enough time, theoretically, for the enterprising young couple to indulge their desire for instant gratification, or, if they lived in a typically conservative neighborhood, to unhook her brassiere.

Is it any wonder then that the album *Johnny Mathis' Greatest Hits* was on the Billboard charts almost forever and is to this day one of the all-time LP best sellers?

"At The Hop," by Singer–Medora–White, 1957

Plenty of guys were too chicken to ask a girl to dance, especially at school dances where the boys stood on one side of the gym, stiff in their new suits, and the girls kicked off their shoes and danced with each other. Somehow it was all right for a girl to dance with another girl, but it would be a good ten years before boys would begin dancing with boys. You went to dances anyway, every Friday night, mainly to hang around the bandstand and pretend to be friends with the drummer.

Boys who didn't know how to dance usually banded together to sneer at those who did—just as on the street the corner bunch tossing a ball around would tease one of their own who passed by all dressed up, with a girl, obviously on a date. To non-dancers the dancers were called "queers," although few had ever contemplated the meaning or practical application of the term. "Queers" were also guys who wore suits to school, who got the highest grades, who knew how to talk to girls without squirming. On the other hand, as the years went by and one by one the corner boys defected (each having been secretly taking cha-cha lessons for the better part of a year), it was often the "queers" who were left playing stoopball on the night of the junior prom.

The dance variations came and went—the Lindy, the Slop, the Phillie Slouch—and though you might watch "American Bandstand" religiously, the art of dancing still seemed the product of another culture. Those who mastered it gained honored admittance into young adulthood, while the footloose, the ungainly, the out-of-step, were doomed to dance alone in perpetual adolescence. The popular boys and girls who knew how to dance would surely move just as easily through the other martial arts of maturity: the art of driving a car, the art of going away to college, the advanced art of intercourse. And then, in 1961, Chubby Checker did "The Twist."

The twist changed the course of modern dancing. First, the dancers stood so far apart that it was no longer really necessary to *have* a partner. The concept of asking a girl to dance (and thus being accepted or horribly rejected) also lost meaning— any girl would accept a twist, because she didn't have to come within ten feet of you. Gone was the communication between boy and girl as in the fox-trot (which you'd finally learned five years too late) where you could tell how much she liked you by how close to her she let you dance. The twist was a solitary dance—a dance of alienation. There has been many a twist I have finished only to find my partner nowhere in sight, having slipped out through a ladies-room window during the drum solo. A man and woman who have twisted together have been less intimate than any two strangers caught in the same subway rush hour.

Unfortunately, in 1961 we were headlong into the Cult of Youth and somehow the twist was picked up as its symbol—it had liberated dancing from its old formal structure; it was a dance with virtually no rules. And in its future incarnations the twist turned dancing into an individual performance sport, like gymnastics, where each dancer is in competition with everyone else on the floor, going through unimaginable contortions and feats of self-torture undreamed of in the primitive days of 1957 when Danny and the Juniors in their sloppy, fat suits first invited us to "The Hop."

"Sweet Little Sixteen," by Chuck Berry, 1958

In 1958 we had our first song about the girls who would later come to be known as Groupies. Young ladies of approximately age sixteen who kept scrapbooks of their favorite rock star in action . . . who diminished the egos of their boyfriends by constantly comparing them to Elvis . . . who lined the streets in front of Brooklyn Paramounts across the country to see their heartthrobs perform . . . who screamed to the heavens while dangling from balconies in the great theater . . . who stalked the stage doors well into the night in the quest of a "famed autograph" . . . who were known to rip the clothes off a rocker's back . . . who would think nothing of entering the star's hotel room, posing as a bellhop, to steal his pillow and aftershave . . . and who dreamed of nothing less.

Frank Sinatra had our mothers. Elvis brought our girl friends and sisters to new and inspired heights of frenzy. But it was Chuck Berry, with his lyrics, who probably did more to promote and identify and extol the Groupie craze than anyone before or since. It developed from there to such a point that in later years it would almost become a pursuable alternate life-style for many young girls.

What the song did for the aspiring pop star is something else again, for it launched full-blown what is still the prevailing fantasy of the rock 'n' roll life, where hero-starved Little Sixteens chase around the country after the pop star, attend to his every whim, then fall by the roadside when the band pulls up stakes and the hero hits the highway. As each generation of Groupie gets successively more daring, we have a situation where fourteen-year-old girls—as typified in the pages of *Star Magazine*—have become Hollywood's latest sex symbols, and king-stud Mick Jagger can write a song called "Star Fucker" (although he can't get it on the radio), showing us that the rock 'n' roll fantasy remains alive and is being nourished by the myth-makers of our age—the pop songwriters.

The other side of this experience, the struggling musician himself, has been dealt with in at least a half dozen classic songs. Chuck Berry in "Johnny B. Goode" (1958) gave us perhaps the archetypal natural rocker. Bill Parsons told of the star machine in "All American Boy" (1959), with tongue in cheek . . . but Roger McGuinn and Chris Hillman with "So You Want To Be A Rock 'n' Roll Star?" got downright cynical, if not bitter. John Sebastian's "Boredom" was mild in its acceptance of the traveling life . . . but Neil Young's "Out Of My Mind" was a cry of desperation. Recently the rock experience has again been summed up, this time by Kevin Johnson in "Rock 'n' Roll (I Gave You The Best Years Of My Life)."

"Yakety Yak," by Leiber and Stoller, 1958

It took a while to realize just how much parents hated rock 'n' roll. They said it was all noise, horrible, suggestive music; the lyrics were unintelligible, senseless at best. They waited impatiently for their kids to grow up—and into a mature appreciation of Broadway standard pop music, the gin and Geritol sound. Or at least to try to be nicer to Eddie Fisher and Pat Boone. When the kids refused they were told to take out the garbage for a week.

Saying that rock 'n' roll was all noise was the same as saying that anyone who greased his hair was a juvenile delinquent. (By this time everyone greased his hair, even bashful chaps who *still* hadn't spoken to girls.) Parents, however, had a lot at stake: the whole world of music they'd grown up with. All those romantic sentiments and slickly phrased love affairs their writers had given them were noisily being trod upon by rebellious youth.

Youth couldn't accept their music; it was too removed from the real world. The real world was the bedrock earthiness of "Don't you step on my blue suede shoes," the unflinching candor of "yip yip yip yip yip yip yip yip, mum mum mum mum mum mum . . ," the fearless "ting tang walla walla bing bang," the racy "Splish splash, I was takin' a bath," and summed up perhaps by the monumental "Why must I be a teen-ager in love?" Things like that had just never been said before in quite the same way.

This is not to discount the fact that some of the greatest moments of teen-age life came on the wings of pure, mad rock 'n' roll noise, brought to you at the highest volume the neighbors would allow. While lying back in your room (or your part of the room) listening to some choice goodie it was not hard to imagine yourself being as noisy and fearless as the music, as the hoods and hicks and blacks and Italians who made it. Rock 'n' roll gave this opportunity—parents took it away; they had a different program, another direction planned, a safe route, not too far from home, a dull life that was everyone's lot sooner or later.

But if rock 'n' roll could exist against their wishes and if kids could be hoods just by greasing their hair, then perhaps parents weren't as all-knowing as they seemed. And life might not be so preplanned. In fact, there could be incredible life-styles waiting out there. Futures beyond the imaginings. Extraordinary challenges.

"Yakety Yak" went for the jugular. It told of how trapped children were by their parents, by their youth—you couldn't even get into the bowling alley unless you were sixteen! Maybe tomorrow they wouldn't take that kind of garbage anymore. In the meantime it was songs like "Yakety Yak" that gave them their first true voice, and perhaps prevented another generation from going silent.

"Teen Angel," by JNR–Surrey, 1960

On February 3, 1959, a plane went down carrying Buddy Holly, Ritchie Valens, and J. P. Richardson (The Big Bopper). The reason this tragedy has since taken on epic, if not legendary overtones, is that it gave the rock 'n' roll generation its first real taste of its own mortality. Until that point they were fearless, indestructible, and expected to live forever. Then, in one swipe, three soldiers were gone.

As an idol James Dean had always belonged to the movie crowd. He was a Hollywood Elvis and when he was killed in 1955 the generation was too young to mourn. Most kids didn't go to the movies more than once a week—they cost a fortune, even if you could still manage to sneak in for children's rates. Radio was free; rock 'n' roll didn't come with matrons throwing you out of the theater for making wisecracks during the love scenes.

Buddy Holly was a skinny kid with glasses, yet he had the nerve to sing, "If we ever part, well *I'll* leave *you!*" He gave the meek a chance to be snotty. Had he lived his rancor might even have surpassed that of Bob Dylan. In fact, it is possible that Dylan himself acquired much of his venomous attitude toward women from an early diet of Buddy Holly (plus a few rotten blind dates).

Ritchie Valens and The Big Bopper capitalized mainly

through their union in death with Holly. Valens had a hit on the charts the day he died ("Oh Donna"), but the depth of his talent would never be known. The Big Bopper was a Texas deejay who scored with "Chantilly Lace" in 1958. Still, they had been up there with Buddy, so they must have been all right. And they went down with Buddy . . . and were gone in a flash.

The preoccupation with death had surfaced before the crash. Jody Reynolds sang "Endless Sleep" in 1958. Thomas Wayne's "Tragedy" had already been released in 1959. The theme would continue to be popular even after the crash was a distant memory, as in "Patches" in 1962. But it was in the year 1960, an otherwise hopeful year, that we were fairly inundated with songs about or ending in death.

Tales like Marty Robbins' "El Paso," "Running Bear" (as written by the same ill-fated Richardson), and "Tell Laura I Love Her," perpetuated the myth of death as an heroic way out and the subsequent worship of the deceased.

The classic of the lot was "Teen Angel." This dirge concerned the sad fate of a young girl so deeply in love that she failed to notice a passenger train bearing down upon her as she rushed back to her boyfriend's jalopy, stalled on the railroad tracks, to retrieve the high school ring he had given her minutes before. Within an instant, before her lover's grief stricken eyes, she is demolished. The story is told as a flashback, with the lover in the present asking his Teen Angel if she safely made it to heaven and whether he can start dating other girls yet.

The lyrics of this song could have been taken straight from page 87 of any city's Sunday news and would be rewritten many times in a world of adolescent joyrides, eleven to a backseat, ending in tragedy and suicide pacts written in blood by doomed lovers, of which the history of teen-age is riddled.

But the generation was nothing if not resilient. It was hard to keep them down for the count. In fact, by 1962 a new Buddy Holly was already on the scene in the person of Tommy Roe, whose song "Sheila" sounded like a carbon copy of the dearly departed hero.

"Those Oldies But Goodies (Remind Me Of You)," by Politi and Curinga, 1961

By 1961 many were approaching high school graduation and already looking back on rock 'n' roll as a source of nostalgia. Parents assured their teen-agers that once out into the serious world of college, the army, or career, rock 'n' roll would at last be revealed as a trivial adolescent passion. Well, if that was true, at least there were the memories. Everyone had a vast body of history from which to pluck golden moments—an instant newspaper of their life and times, quickly recalling person and place in the space of three minutes.

We had gone from "Blue Suede Shoes" to "Tan Shoes And Pink Shoelaces." We had noticed "Short Shorts" and gazed a little more closely at "Itsy Bitsy Teenie Weenie Yellow Polka Dot Bikini." At night we still cruised the highway in the shotgun seat calling out to cheerleaders named "Sherry," "Suzie Darlin'," "Denise," and "Mary Ann"—searching either for that "Dream Lover" or just to avoid another "Lonely Weekend."

The generation was momentarily suspended at sixteen, from "Sweet Little Sixteen" to "Sixteen Candles" to "You're Sixteen" to "Happy Birthday Sweet Sixteen," not to mention "Sixteen Reasons" and "Sixteen Tons." In the meantime, rock 'n' roll had spread out. It had entered the Italian neighborhood with Dion and the Belmonts, Frankie Avalon, Annette Funicello, and Connie Francis; the Jewish neighborhood with Neil Sedaka and Howie Greenfield, two guys from Brooklyn who wrote a song about a girl they knew named Carol Klein, who went with a chemistry student named Gerry. The song was a hit, "Oh Carol." A few years later Carol would come to be known as Carole King, the Gerry Goffin–Carole King combination—hitmakers extraordinare of the sixties.

In 1962 Bobby Vinton sang a generation down the graduation

aisle with "Roses Are Red," and Diane Renay sent off a contingent of servicemen with "Blue, Navy Blue," as did the Shirelles with "Soldier Boy." Everyone rode "Telstar" into the future.

Although enjoyed in groups, rock 'n' roll was also a private matter—certain legendary highs experienced alone, maybe on the roof, catching Detroit on a clear night, or that station up in Canada. Sounds in the air linking you to brothers and sisters seen and unseen. Roy Orbison was crying for them as he did for you. It was also a chance refrain, heard once or twice and never again, like a girl's face seen on a crosstown bus drifting slowly out of view with the changing of the light—"Jo-ann," by the Playmates; "Believe Me," by the Royal Teens. To each his own obsession.

By 1962 all of the great subjects had been handled classically by our talented writers, some of them peers. But what no one could know was that rock 'n' roll would graduate too, would accompany the generation as it confronted the next world. And what a world, what a confrontation!

As the Rooftop Singers advised in 1962 to all those who would listen: "Walk right in, sit right down, Daddy let your mind roll on . . ." ("Walk Right In," by Darling & Suanoe).

DOC POMUS

Doc Pomus (with Mort Shuman), Jerry Leiber (with Mike Stoller), Chuck Berry, Fats Domino, and a handful of others were the seminal figures during the transition period from rhythm and blues into rock 'n' roll. While Berry and Domino were essentially singer/songwriters, Pomus and Leiber made their livings ghostwriting words for Elvis Presley and the many

acts that followed his glittering footsteps into the brave new world of pop music.

In person Pomus is a cross between Doctor John and Burl Ives, a big man, bearded, confined to a wheelchair. Behind the scenes in the music business he is truly a venerated figure, the pro's pro, a veteran of many bags. In the late fifties his creations spurred such groups as Dion and the Belmonts and the Drifters to huge success. When the Beatles arrived in 1964, leading the British revolution in a takeover of the Brill Building, ancient gathering place for New York City staff songwriters, Doc and the others broke ranks and disappeared. He never gave up writing, however, the hits just stopped coming—an example of the winds that blow hot and cold in the songwriting arena.

The interview with Doc Pomus took place in an uptown Manhattan coffeehouse. It was a spirited discussion, lasting well into the evening dinner rush.

"Early success is tough to live with—success is tough to live with anytime, it's almost as tough as failure. My experience has been it's always tougher for me to take success because most of my life has been filled with failure and I found it very easy to live with. It was only when I started getting successful—I was in my thirties—that I found it impossible. I must have blown a half a million dollars, all because of one thing—I couldn't cope with success. It's a madness. You know, up until the time I was thirty-two years old my good years were when I was able to buy a suit, you know, this was a real good year. Then suddenly you're going into a store and having ten made to order.

"I've gone through the other side too. What happens is that you start imagining you know what a hit record is and suddenly that song that you swore is a hit song isn't a hit, and it destroys you, absolutely destroys you.

"The thing that scared me most, from a personal viewpoint, is that I had a marriage that broke up and I got out of the business. So I had to go back to writing because I had blown all my money and the first couple of months I didn't know what the hell I was doing. It was a really bad period. But when I got back into it I really thought I was doing some good tunes, but nothing was happening and it went on and on . . . for a couple of years. Now when I look back on those songs I realize there was nothing wrong with them, it was just a question of today the markets are so limited.

"But the scariest thing is when you think you've found the formula and suddenly you realize there's no such animal. And no matter what anybody else will say, there's so much luck involved. When you're on a streak you never even think of it. Catch almost anybody who's got a number of hit songs and he'll show you fifty songs that you'll think are just as good that nothing happened to. As for myself, almost without exception, every hit song I've ever written has been rejected by ten or fifteen artists. I mean rejected seriously, where an artist will say, how can you think that this song is going to be a hit? So by this time I don't say a word. I just write them and do what I can with them.

"Once we wrote two songs for Bobby Rydell and his A 'n' R man rejected one of them. Now there was a rock 'n' roll show and we went to it and Jimmy Clanton was working there and I told Jimmy, we wrote a song for you. The song was originally titled 'Go Bobby Go,' so we changed it to 'Go Jimmy Go,' and he recorded it. He never knew till years later that it wasn't for him. And somewhere there's a tape where Bobby Rydell is singing 'Go Bobby Go.' So that's why it's hard for me to take this whole thing seriously."

I asked how he got into songwriting.

"Originally I was off and on a writer. At times I've been a music critic. Different times I've written articles. And I've had some fiction published. But mostly I was a singer and I used to write a lot of songs for blues singers like Joe Turner and Ray Charles.

"Funny, it was always easier for me to make a living writing than it was singing. I used to write to survive because I was always making records that weren't successful. Finally, when I was about thirty, I started to realize that singing was a losing battle, so I began to concentrate on writing. And two or three years later I suddenly started getting hits all over the place.

"What happens is you're forced to write. It's something you can't explain. I mean you just write because you have to write. I don't think success or lack of success has anything to do with it. Anybody who says they write for any other reason is just lying.

"The first song I wrote that made nationwide noise was 'Youngblood,' by the Coasters. The first song you could call a rock 'n' roll song was something by Fabian, 'I'm a Man.' I sometimes get confused in the chronological order because at that time or soon afterwards what happened was that Morty and myself had eight hits going at one time on the charts.

"In the old days there were always people to help you. Leiber and Stoller were a great help to me, fantastic fellows. Also Otis Blackwell. Otis introduced me to Hill and Range publishing, and they were the first publishers I signed up with. Leiber and Stoller helped me get a Lavern Baker recording and for a fact they helped me in rewriting certain songs.

"There's no fun in it anymore. It used to be a great community, the projects were interesting and you worked mostly with the artists. If you wrote with somebody you always knew the publisher was giving advances. Like if Leiber and Stoller had an act they'd call you up and tell you that they wanted to work and then they'd help you—not trying to get a piece of the song; it was all for the product. If it was a good product we were all happy.

"Today there's such hostility. I've only become aware of it in the last few years and I think it's true in every facet of our existence. It's competitive in the wrong kind of way. I know every time you try to do something, for instance, with a producer, if somebody else loses out on a session, my God, the guy won't talk to you.

"I still make a very good living. It's not that I'm complaining because I'm having survival problems. There's just no fun in it anymore.

"I'll tell you this, from a numerical point of view, there are better songwriters today, I would say, than ten years ago. At that time there were a handful of good songwriters. Now there's a double handful. Also younger people today are very talented. In the past I would say that the good songwriters were ten years older.

"You know, I met John Lennon last year at a BMI dinner, in fact we spent the whole dinner together. One of the biggest kicks I had was when Lennon told me that one of the first songs the Beatles ever did was a song I wrote called 'Lonely Avenue.' You never know if other writers are aware of you. And he was telling me originally all they wanted to do was reach a point, like Morty and myself or like Carole King and Gerry, where they could make enough money to survive writing songs. Then when all that success happened; look at him— he can't cope."

I asked Doc if he had any opinions as to why so many of this generation's talented songwriters seemed to be dying out early, disappearing or drying up for long periods of time. In this respect I mentioned Dylan, Gerry Goffin, Laura Nyro, Tim Hardin, James Taylor, Phil Ochs, and Jimmy Webb.

"Most of these young kids haven't paid the dues. You have to pay a certain amount of dues before it all comes together. They're so young and success comes so fast, I think that's what happens. But eventually, if they can reach a point in their development where things can fuse, they can still turn out fantastically. But I think that's what accounts for so many creative people suffering through kind of a long interim period where they're not creating. I think Dylan just went through it and I'm sure success had a lot to do with it because—I don't have to tell you—the stimuli for creativity are such odd things and I think if it's not based on so many of the things that it has to be based on, then somewhere along the line there's a lag."

I asked about his own working habits.

"I write all the time. At first I used to write the melodies and lyrics, and the funny thing is I considered myself more of a melody writer than a lyric writer. Eventually I became a lyric writer, not even involved with melodies at all. That's why, when I hear some of my old songs, I can't believe I wrote both, because it's a whole different frame of reference. I couldn't visualize myself being alone writing a song now. There's a certain type of solitary thing that I can't do anymore. I just have to be with somebody in a room and keep throwing ideas back and forth.

"Generally I've always worked the same way. I've always had a premise and we worked on the premise. It would be a title or an idea or approximately a title, and then you'd get some pictures. Whenever I have an idea I always write it out, but I never know beforehand whether it's very commercial or not. When I'm through I know if it's a good song or if it isn't a good song. Some of my favorite songs would have no reason at all to be hits, they're just ideas that I liked that I worked through.

"It's mostly a question of projection. I don't know what the subconscious mechanisms are, but right away something happens where I just think in terms of doing the idea as well as I can. The whole thing is communicating, you know, and I have to say if the song is good enough for me and I like it and I can understand it, I have to be egotistical enough to imagine it'll be understood somewhere else. But sometimes you get thrown. Every once in a while I'll do a song that I think is clear, with a good message, and the publisher will have no idea what it's about.

"I've written some very personal songs. 'Lonely Avenue,' that Ray Charles recorded, is about myself. And I have a couple of personal ones that nobody has seen except the publisher. But that's the nature of the process. When I get an idea sometimes it's personal, sometimes it's an idea that's out of context. I just write the idea.

"But I'll tell you this, if you don't have a good melody I don't give a damn how good your lyric is. Whereas if you have a real strong melody sometimes the lyrics can subordinate. Also, you're driven by a good melody, you'll write better lyrics. I got spoiled because the fellow I was working with all those years, Mort Shuman, was absolutely brilliant and it's just a shame that he doesn't want to be involved with popular songs anymore.

"So, unfortunately, you're at the mercy of your co-writer, which has bothered me for the last four or five years. Let me put it to you this way: Doing this for so many years, you develop a facility, and generally if I'm under contract to a firm they'll put me with somebody who might not have even had a song published, let alone a hit song. And I'll be about three times as fast as he is and then I start getting depressed when there are lags along the way.

"I like to work with a song in parts. I'm not really geared to write the complete song. But I wind up writing about two-thirds of the song anyway simply because I'm working with someone who can't do anything. Or else you're subject to all the hangups of the cat. You know, if they don't have proper bowel movements that morning, forget about it. In my experience ninety percent of the guys you sit with, before you can actually do the first note, you gotta listen to their stories for about two hours. I'm just not in the mood for it anymore. And this is also with people who have great reputations. It's bad enough going through it with them, but imagine when you have to go through it with an amateur.

"I remember there was a time about five years ago when I

was under contract to Screen Gems and they had some heavy writers there and this one guy came over to write with me and before we got a song going he spent two hours playing all his hits for me. I couldn't believe it. I knew all his hits and he knew all my hits, but he had to go through them all for two hours. We never wrote a song.

"But generally I like to relate, to work with somebody where you're throwing ideas around, cause I like to edit the melody. Sometimes you can look at a melody so objectively that you can see an extraneous part to it and just throw it out, and the melody writer appreciates it. By the same token I may do something lyrically where the guy will say, if you cut out a couple of words it'll help the melody. So I've always found it easy to work that way.

"I write three or four times a week. I've been guilty; I haven't been to the office in about three or four months. I'm under contract to Twentieth Century. I haven't gone there only because I find that very often you get involved in political situations there. There's always factions in an office. I can't wade through all that bullshit. If I have an appointment there I go, but generally I try to keep my appointments away from the office. So we write at my apartment. When we finish, the music man writes a lead sheet and we go and make a cheap demo, which we then send to the Coast, for Twentieth Century's perusal.

"You see, what it is, also, you always have a reputation in the areas where you've been successful. I don't consider myself a rock 'n' roll songwriter. I think blues comes easiest to me. The last group I had before I stopped singing had King Curtis and Mickey Baker in it. But I just haven't had the occasion to write blues. I write show tunes as easy as I write rock 'n' roll. I think if you're a songwriter you can do all of them.

"The only thing I'm a little skeptical about in regard to today's writers, is could they write the gamut? That's the only thing. There are so many talents who are suspect only because they're limited talents in the sense that they can only work in certain areas. I think the function of a songwriter is to be able to write every kind of song. In recent years I've gotten very involved with country and western music. There's another facet of creativity that I hadn't been involved with. So now I have a capacity for writing that kind of song.

"You see, when you're writing constantly—and I'm writing constantly—you have to mature in your writing. You have a greater facility and you get into other areas. I know I find myself writing more introspectively. It's simply the nature of the times today. I've been influenced by what's going on as much as any songwriter.

"And I'll tell you something else; it's not necessarily true that the best songs are the ones that come easy. Some of the best songs I've written were hard to write, others were easy. 'Save The Last Dance For Me' I think was written in about thirty minutes, and yet another tune we wrote for the Drifters, 'I Count The Tears,' took us two weeks to write."

I felt compelled to ask him about perhaps his most famous single record, "Teenager In Love," by Dion and the Belmonts. A song which once had three different versions in the British Top Ten during the same week. Certainly one of the landmark songs of adolescence.

"I don't even remember writing 'Teenager In Love.' It was an assignment. We wrote the other side of that record too and I always liked it better. It was a song called 'I've Cried Before.' We had a song that we'd already written called 'Teenager In Love,' and Dion liked the lyric to it and wanted us to change the melody. So we just changed the melody."

A closing comment.

"Well, I tell you, I find songwriting more interesting now than I ever did. Writing per se is more interesting. It's less fun, but more interesting."

GERRY GOFFIN

Along with his first wife, composer Carole King, Gerry Goffin has been responsible for some of the most memorable and enduring music of the early sixties. Working out of Don Kirshner's tiny Aldon Music factory, the same publishing house which spawned lyricists Cynthia Weil ("Blame It On The Bossa Nova"), Howard Greenfield ("Happy Birthday Sweet Sixteen"), Lee Kolber ("Patches"), Gerry Goffin practically wrote the scenario for a generation that cruised the highway in beat-up roadsters, hung out in team jackets at drive-in burger stands or Carvels, and found love to the tune of the Top Forty radio stations in the back seat parked beyond the empty lots down alongside the swamp.

Working out of New York City his lyrics reflected a street sense, timed to the rhythm of the traffic lights, backed by the consistent, pulsing beat of the rattling subway underneath. It was a time when the City was still considered the place to be, where thousands of young men and women hitched with their high school graduation money, their one good suit, to seek their fortunes—the Big Apple.

In 1973, ten years after he and Carole King were signed to Screen Gems for a reported $100,000-a-year advance, Gerry Goffin's name means little more than nostalgia to a new generation of rock fans. Although renditions of his old songs still come out regularly (and make the Top Ten!), he and Carole King have split up, professionally and maritally. Both have remained creative, however, with Carole becoming a superstar in a solo role and Gerry, after a layoff, emerging with a new partner, Barry Goldberg, a new hit song "I've Got To Use My Imagination," recorded by Gladys Knight and the Pips, and an album

of songs—on which he sings for the first time—entitled *It Ain't Exactly Entertainment* (Adelphi Records).

After quite a while tracking down the reclusive Mr. Goffin, I finally interviewed him in the offices of Screen Gems Music, where he is known among the secretaries as a figure of legend and mystery. Goffin was very offhand about his career, hesitant about any generalizations in regard to songwriting, and ambivalent about his accumulated body of songs, their impact and their worth.

"Irwin Schuster [head of Screen Gems Music] gave me a list of songs I wrote and I can't believe some of the titles."

Does it seem like a whole other person wrote them?

"I *know* I wrote them, that's what hurts."

It is this half-kidding, evasive tone which Gerry adopted for most of the interview. Some examples:

When did you start taking lyric writing seriously?

"I never took it seriously."

Do you think youth plays a great part in the productivity of a songwriter?

"Stupidity helps."

After a while, though, we did get down to specifics.

"I'm not gonna say whether my songs were good or bad. It's pretty good to be successful at songwriting. If the people like them that's fine and I'm happy. There was a time when I used to cringe hearing them; now I don't anymore because I figure it was that time and it was okay. I mean, you've got to realize when I started writing songs. There's been several revolutions that have taken place in pop music since then, and I think they were all improvements. I've always thought, any way you looked at it, that the changes have been for the better.

"I mean, it's better than having assignments. Groups are writing now for their own personal feelings—it's a whole different thing. To me that's a little more honest, not that I didn't enjoy what I was doing."

What was it like in the old days?

"In those days it was write a song for this group or write a song for so and so. That was our job, Carole and I, and it was a lot of fun. When you're young you don't mind doing that so much. When you get a little older you sort of rebel against that and you get a tendency to want not to write to a market. I can't write under deadlines anymore . . . but I respect people who can.

"Right now I'm just writing what I feel like writing and I keep changing. If I want to write something commercial I don't see anything wrong with it. If I want to write a song that I feel personally, I don't see anything wrong with that either."

It is interesting to note, in this context, that Goffin's solo album, a package containing sixteen originals, has in it not one typical "hit" song. A good percentage of the songs could be termed "protest"—a type of writing which was most popular from 1963 to 1968, that period of time when Goffin was struggling to turn out three gems for the Drifters, the Shirelles, and the Monkees. Also on the album are quite a few lyrics in which Goffin probably reveals himself to a greater extent than he will in any interview. One in particular, "Everything and Nothing," seems, quite adeptly, to describe his rather ambiguous feelings as to his past achievements and his current prospects.

"In the last six months I've been in a slump, so right now I can't imagine putting a song together. When I was younger I could write everyday, but it all gets corny after a while. It's been a lot of years of writing and a lot has been said and written. I've written a couple of thousand songs. I tell you, I write a lot more songs that people don't use—about fifty to one.

"Sometimes you write just because there's nothing else to do. Last year I wrote forty songs in forty days. But I've been pretty drained since I finished my album. I don't think anyone should be drained that much, but I certainly haven't thought of anything to write about since then.

"There's also another thing. There's a certain magic that some records have and that some records don't have and that's not a quality you can capture unless everything is going right, and that's something that comes and goes and there's no formula for it.

"I'm talking about even at a record session. There are so many personalities involved, so many variables. Sometimes you could write a mediocre song and it becomes a big hit—it's really hard to talk about."

Gerry Goffin was born in Brooklyn, as was Carole King (*née* Klein). They met at Queens College where Gerry was advancing reluctantly toward a career in chemistry. But he had always written songs.

"I started writing songs when I was eight years old. I mean just lyrics, like some kind of game in my head. I'd think of them as songs—they'd have a kind of inane melody. Sometimes I would sing the melodies over chords, but they were pretty horrible. In fact, even after we made it, no one recorded them.

"When there was sort of a completed melody and a whole structure and I'd write to that, those seemed to be better songs. Many of them were written simultaneously, sort of one line at a time. When you're writing something good it always seems to be easy. Anytime it took me a long time to write a song it usually wasn't too good a song.

"When I say good I mean something that's right, marketable, that has something to say. It has to go through a lot of different ears; different people have to decide if it's something that people want to hear. If it gets on the radio and if people want to hear it, they buy it. That's how I thought I could tell if a song was going to be a hit or not, or how big a hit it would be—by listening to it on the radio. I never listened at home; I used to always listen in the car. I don't know, it was just something about the resonance of the car radio, usually with the good records you caught the sound of a hit single."

I asked him how he felt about the songs and songwriters of today.

"Randy Newman has his own approach. He's probably the most uncorrupted lyricist there is. I like him. I like Joni Mitchell; she represents some sort of sophistication in what she writes about. I can appreciate them and I can appreciate the Chi-lites. It's nice to turn on your radio and get good music.

"I mean, first it was just sort of pop lyrics, then all of a sudden poetry got involved, and there's a big difference between being a pop lyricist and being a poet—which blew my head a whole lot. Being a poet is a lot harder, it's really work. I had a desire to write that kind of song—to be a poet—but I wasn't able to, so I gave it up.

"What's happening today musically to me is pretty amazing. I think Dylan is very good, and there's a magic there too. I never could do [protest songs] very well. I mostly did it very straight forward, but I agreed with everything that was said. I don't see how it's possible to dislike that kind of songwriting.

"After the Beatles started to grow and get real good, it suddenly didn't appear that going in and writing songs for whoever you were writing songs for was the way anymore."

How do his own songs sound on the radio these days?

"No matter what you write it always sounds good on the radio, so they sound fine. But not as fine as Chuck Berry. I think Chuck Berry wrote the best lyrics to describe what it was like in teen-age America in those days. I think his was a more accurate picture than mine. I didn't realize how good his lyrics were—because I didn't listen to lyrics much, I mean I just sort of enjoyed them—until I got a job and had to write them everyday.

"To simplify it. It's a nice job, having to write. Being a lyricist is a pretty nice job. It's not hard, and if people like my songs I'm very happy. I mean, that's the way I feel."

PART TWO

Newport Generation:

1961–1965

(The Cause)

"A Hard Rain's Gonna Fall," by Bob Dylan, 1961

Allen Ginsburg wrote the poem "Howl!" in 1955. Jack Kerouac published *On the Road* in 1956. Lawrence Ferlinghetti's *A Coney Island of the Mind* came out in 1958 in the farewell period of the Beat Generation. Beatniks hung out in coffeehouses in San Francisco's North Beach and New York's Greenwich Village. They were into poetry, jazz, the hipster life on the edge of the street, dope, open sex, and the open road. They were the intellectual who celebrated the spontaneous existence of the small-time thug, the con-man poet, and truck-driver philosopher who traveled across the country at breakneck speeds in search of kicks, meaning, and new routes to nirvana.

By 1960 most of them had vanished back into the American landscape which had produced them, back with their tattered passionate manuscripts to dim rooms in coldwater flats on the outskirts of the slums to work in solitude. Ginsburg went to India, Kerouac to New Jersey to stay with his mother, Ferlinghetti dug in and opened up the City Lights bookstore in North Beach. Except for a midnight poetry reading, a Bowery jazz concert, an encounter in a literary bar here and there, Greenwich Village fell silent. And then, in 1961, Bob Dylan blew into town.

Dylan was a middle-class Jew from Minnesota, brought up on country and western music, Hank Williams, Chicago rhythm and blues, Buddy Holly, and the rock 'n' roll experience. Dylan Thomas provided the inspiration for his stage name (from the mundane Zimmerman)—making him pleasing to the young intelligentsia. His professed idol was Woody Guthrie, one of the premier folk balladeers of the Depression, who often took up the cause of the common man laid low by poverty. The latent radicals saw in Dylan a continuation of the Guthrie legend. Woody's songs were about outlaws and tramps; Dylan's songs gave voice to the outlaw/tramp. Eventually he would come to use Dylan Thomas imagery in rhythm and blues songs (sung in a country and western drawl) concerning the rock 'n' roll experience. From the start he had all the bases covered.

Dylan as a rule-breaker set the standard for nearly as large a portion of the populace as Elvis had before him, but whereas with Elvis when you peeled away the flaming rebel image, you found a God-fearing, mom-loving, good old flag-waving boy who said "shucks"—and who, like the rest of the kids would grow up to be a fine upstanding solid citizen, none the worse for his wayward youth—with Dylan you found underneath his universal backwoods hillbilly mystic image a series of other images, each as devious and compelling as the next. There was the sneering child-prodigy, the rustic poet-genius, the baby-faced beatnik, even America's own orphan prophet. He changed colors as he did moods, changed autobiographies with the skill of a short-story writer, creating himself as a different character each week in full view of the unknowing public. When a final accounting of Dylan's worth as an artist and his importance to his time is set forth (not here) it may perhaps come as a surprise to note that his greatest achievement will have been the creation of that dazzling succession of personas which came to be known collectively the world over as Bob Dylan.

"The Times They Are A-Changing," by Bob Dylan, 1963
Dylan was a college dropout long before it became the fashion. He journeyed east with his guitar to visit Woody Guthrie, who lay dying in a New Jersey hospital, to play his idol some songs. Years later Dylan would become the idol, the standard against which other young middle-class dreamers would measure themselves, their creations, and their lives. Dylan symbolized hope by publicly seizing his life from the establishment (parents, school, army, career) and making his fantasy world into a reality on the strength of his dream, his wit, his vision, and his talent. Others, hearing the news, would be stirred to action.

For many, Dylan was too much to take at first. His songs were raw, bitter, plainly offensive to those who were brought up on rock 'n' roll. While everyone could feel for "Teen Angel," only a handful were ready for Dylan's rendition of "See That My Grave Is Kept Clean." His own "Masters Of War," which was a violent anti-war song, threatened a generation which had grown up saluting the flag and singing "The Star-Spangled Banner" every morning. No one had ever attacked the government in song before. Even Elvis had gone into the service when it was his turn, though everyone hated to see him depart. Dylan was more like the denizens of the Beat Generation, howling his subterranean message to an adolescent public which for the most part had been pretty satisfied with vicarious kicks, living a mini-rebellion through the music. Dylan came upon a stale and placid rock 'n' roll in the early sixties and in one startling chord change, one ragged line of verse, brought it back to the seething street where it had started in the mid-fifties. Once again the music was political, and Dylan's voice was a call to arms.

Early Dylan fans were protective of their idol, defending him against their know-nothing friends who preferred the likes of Peter, Paul, and Mary, whose sweet versions of "Blowin' In The Wind" and "Don't Think Twice" helped to make Dylan a household name. He was their cause, and it was the Dylan issue, for or against, which opened the split within the ranks of the rock 'n' roll youth culture (the first since the R&B fans dropped off in 1956) that, in the following years, would widen to a gulf while the whole country felt the tremors.

Dylan offered indications that the unwavering, straight line down the middle of the road that middle-class parents mapped out might be filled with hidden bends, detours of incalculable miles into uncharted woods and forests. Some clung fearfully to the line, what had become in the sixties the dulling drumbeat of rock 'n' roll; others, recalling "Yakety Yak," threw off their life jackets and swam upstream along with their new scout-master.

"Come To My Bedside," by Eric Andersen, 1964

By 1964 virgins everywhere, male and female, began to doubt

the validity of their status. Middle-class males started to realize
that they might not have to marry the first girl they slept with;
middle-class girls started to question this thing they had been
taught to save until their wedding day. Non-virgins of the time
threw-off their guilt and celebrated instead the pioneering
nature of their actions.

The early liberated woman began showing her face on the
odd college campus, the Bohemian neighborhood East and West.
They were not the obvious low-reputation types with purple
eye shadow, nor were they the loose and desperate kind from
the neighborhood who used sex as a downpayment on the long-
term mortgage of marriage. Instead, these females gave indications of being truly real, the advance guard in the sexual
revolution that was to follow. The archetypal liberated woman
had long straight hair, used little or no makeup, and wore plain
unembroidered shifts (usually handmade) with black net stock-
ings and sandals or white half-sneakers. There were regional
variations of course.

The image of this new woman was carried in countless folksongs of the era and perhaps stemmed from the front cover
photo of Bob Dylan's second album of Bob and his girl walking
down a snowy Greenwich Village street, her long hair blowing
in the wind. My own opinion is that the whole thing started
with Janet Margolin, who played Lisa in the film *David and
Lisa*—the wistful, pure-faced, psychotic folk-music dreamgirl.

How authentic this image was is impossible to verify; however, legend had it that this type of woman was neither a prude
nor promiscuous, merely selective and true to herself. She
needed no elaborate, far-ranging plans to allow herself to have
sex with someone. The folk-music dreamgirl (often a poet or
artist too) could see the soul of her lover, and that was enough.

Sex without ritual tended instead to be the dream of what is
called "the late bloomer," that is, the outcasts and loners who'd
always been unable to play the games required in high school.
While the others were out dancing and driving and making out,

these late bloomers were reading books, developing obscure interests and outlooks, perhaps even writing the poetry which would come to be the new folksongs . . . all the while pondering the soullessness of the modern high-school prince and princess. Bob Dylan wrote, "the losers now will be later to win . . ." and it was the sensibility of folk music that many early social losers would turn to in order to find the strength needed to reverse the trend of their adolescence.

In Eric Andersen's words the American public was made aware of what had previously only been hinted at, suggested, made obvious to kids in code. A new sexual frontier was being forged, a guilt-free attitude emerging from the twisted mire of Western civilization, with virtually no help from adults. Andersen wrote of dropped petticoats, of proud lovers who made love not frantically in the back seat of a car, or obscenely in the last row of the balcony, but in bed (in their *parents'* bed, no less). Andersen himself was an unabashed romantic even at a time when Dylan was a sneering cynic and Phil Ochs was too wrapped up in politics to think about it.

Parents may have always suspected what their kids were up to late at night in the basement (with good old Johnny Mathis *still* playing on the record player), but the new liberation in song lyrics told them what they weren't ready to hear. Soon after that their sons and daughters announced to them point-blank that, at sixteen they were no longer virgins or at twenty-one they were living with their lovers and had no immediate intentions of getting married. With that, sex was taken out of the basement and brought upstairs to the bedroom where it belonged. For the children of the sixties, telling their parents the naked truth may have been the most overt rebellion of all.

"Draft Dodger Rag," by Phil Ochs, 1964

The topic of utmost priority on the minds of every American male between the ages of eighteen and twenty-six was the draft . . . and how to beat it. Once it became obvious that the young men of this generation, unlike others before it, were not going to quietly submit to it, everyone sought to form their own unique escape plan. No night could be restful from then on until that coveted deferment or 4F was safely gotten.

Many men became teachers, that being a legal way out. Quite a few unlikely drones actually took master's degrees in order to buy off the shade for a year or two more. When dependents were a way out, married men impregnated their wives, in order to avoid making them widows. Some with no other alternatives chose Canada; others bravely faced jail sentences. Those who qualified sought conscientious objection. *Everyone* spent anxious hours awaiting their physical.

The draftcard, once a symbol of majority, noble ticket of admission to beer halls and strip joints, became a vile tool of destruction, a passport to oblivion on a one-way charter. Some burned theirs while most stood on the sidelines (or in the beer halls) cheering them on.

When, in 1968, the draft lottery was begun, no nation of young men ever tuned in a horse race with so much at stake. As the numbers were called off we watched our brothers cry in agony or let out sighs of relief powerful enough to float a barge across the Mississippi.

Phil Ochs' "Draft Dodger Rag," stands back to back with Buffy Sainte-Marie's "Universal Soldier," as the two more revealing anti-war songs of the era. Buffy's lyric calls attention to the ageless folly of war, unchanged by time or progress. Each person who allowed himself to go to war had to bear part of the guilt, for without the soldier there could be no war. The generation kept Buffy's words in mind as they set about evading the war machine.

"Draft Dodger Rag," although a satirization of the same immortal fakers, captured the feeling of a generation trying to save itself. Within the song a good number of tactics were pointed up . . . but it barely touched the surface of their survival ingenuity. Dressing up as a female or coming to the physical on LSD worked only until the army doctors caught on. Men with foresight enlisted the aid of their own shrinks to destroy their minds and bodies as quickly as possible. Others started the deterioration process months or even years before their examination date with pills and drugs and strange behavior of all description. This may perhaps account, in part, for the alarming number of catatonic schizophrenics with suicidal tendencies that sprang up in the latter years of the sixties, after the draft was no longer a factor.

Folksinger Arlo Guthrie (son of the late Woody Guthrie) became an instant superstar on the basis of one song, "Alice's Restaurant," a lyric which espoused draft evasion and offered one man's blueprint for doing the same.

"Mr. Tamborine Man," by Bob Dylan, 1964

If rock 'n' roll separated the men from the boys, the solid from the square, the children from the parents, imagine the effect of the evil weed. The stormy history of marijuana has been charted extensively, the cases pro and con, the uses both psychological and medical. However, in the residue of such debate one fact stands clear: The adoption of this plant as the favored stoning method and initiation rite of the young in the mid-sixties threatened to bring the country to a second Prohibition Era and succeeded in making lawbreakers of nearly an entire generation.

Breaking the law was not the most thrilling aspect of smoking pot. Many had already duped the establishment by evading the draft. Clearly the only choice to be made about dope was whether it would wreck your mind, stunt your growth, and destroy your future or not. It was that simple.

Of course, rumor had it that hoods had been smoking dope for years out behind the poolhall on Saturday nights before a big drag race. It was no small-potatoes kick, and as such was worth more than the usual risk. The middle-class person had been warned that one step off the straight and narrow would mean certain annihilation—including staying in school, preparing for a prosperous career, going into the army, and marrying your (virgin) high-school sweetheart upon release. This could all be eternally spoiled if you were to come within a hundred yards of the dreaded weed. It would go down on your *record* for life—this mythical record that someone was keeping on you. We didn't find out *who,* until years later.

It was the knowledge that you could completely ruin everything that your parents had been killing themselves for so that you could have, which made marijuana such a first-class kick. It gave one the opportunity to start over, with no advantages, independent. Instant liberation. (Of course parents could not be talked to on the subject at all, especially when you were stoned.)

So, under their noses, the country turned on. In the space of three or four years in the mid-sixties, nearly everyone sampled a joint or two, and, depending on the quality of the product, got off. And things were never quite the same again. It was not so much that dope altered perceptions (which it did) but that for a lot of people it made them aware they *had* perceptions in the first place. And it was mild! That something so sweet (easier on the draw than your average cigarette) could be so powerful, could inside a few minutes change everything for a few hours, was strong food for fantasy. Here were those extraordinary challenges. Here was the different life rock 'n' roll had promised back in 1958.

The generation quickly divided again, into Those Who Smoked and Those Who Scorned. Mainly, Those Who Smoked attempted to turn on Those Who Scorned, and Those Who Scorned regarded Those Who Smoked as evil, alien, sick, the new degenerates—until a week later when they too crossed the line and realized where it was at. Marijuana was not the evil weed; one puff didn't bring on addiction, tragedy, the long arm of the law. As the converts multiplied and pot took over, instead of the generation, the two prime casualties of the movement were parents and the law. Neither could be respected as authorities as much as before because of the dishonest way they treated the situation.

But at first smokers were in the distinct minority and were made to suffer the wrath of even their peers. Dope came to replace rock 'n' roll as the rallying point for all rebels. However, as rebels, these dope-smoking types were an embarrassment to classify; they were of good breeding, the pride of the neighborhood, the high I.Q. well-motivated young men and women— stoned out of their minds. It was impossible to dismiss them as one might have been able to dismiss the lower-class, leather-jacketed hoods of the fifties. When class-presidents dropped out of school to live in the slums and smoke dope, things got serious. When they started to wear leather jackets too . . . it was time to reevaluate the data.

Soon we started getting a lot of songs written to or about or under the influence of dope. In fact, whenever an adult radio programmer couldn't understand an imagistic lyric, he labeled it a dope song. Thus "Puff, The Magic Dragon," "Walk Right In," and "Mr. Tamborine Man" have come to be thought of as pioneering drug lyrics, although their authors have denied that intent. Songs written while stoned were another matter, much harder to prove. Basically, the early drug songs were of necessity written in code, just as sex lyrics had been for ages. But in 1965 when The Byrds made "Mr. Tamborine Man" a national number one hit, it was time to realize that almost everyone knew the code, and about half that number were sampling the product. The remainder of the sixties would more than bear this out.

"Take Off Your Thirsty Boots," by Eric Andersen, 1964

Many of those who took part in the protest movement, whether marching against the war or for civil rights, did so with a camp reunion mentality. Here was the chance to pick up a nice folk-music dreamgirl, to hear the latest protest songs, to mingle among those of a similar persuasion (still not as popular back in the neighborhood). The speeches were boring to them, repetitive; the marches themselves of dubious effect. Who could change the government, after all? The government, as we learned in the fifties, was up on Mount Olympus—that great dome visited on high-school trips—remote, untouchable. But the miles were marched, the speeches listened to . . . so that, eventually, the folksingers could perform.

These were mostly young people, the style setters of the new breed, in dungarees and scuffed boots—leather boots (just when you had finally broken in your Italian pointy-toe dancing shoes!). The songs they played were not your typical three-minute Tin Pan Alley slush, not even the still-stylish rock 'n' roll. These were fierce tirades, long, painful personal statements, ballads in direct language concerning relevant topics of the day —Phil Ochs' "Mississippi Find Yourself Another Country To Be Part Of," Buffy Sainte-Marie's "Now That The Buffalo's Gone," and everybody's favorite Uncle Pete Seeger's "Big Muddy." Here was the deposed student council leader lately taken to smoking pot, the renegade ex-college editor proving one didn't need a degree to amount to something. The folk-singers seemed to be the exciting minds of the generation, living out the fantasies of escape and commitment the rest of us provided them. The singers wrote and sang, the audience remained in class, getting out for a demonstration only about once or twice a month.

Politics was on everyone's mind. The Vietnam War could no longer be ignored. The draft threatened with each morning's mail. By the act of smoking dope you were a criminal in the eyes of the law. What matter then your own hangups—date night blues, can't get the car—with the world in such perilous shape? Rock 'n' roll ceased being relevant; it became part of the problem.

And down South black men were still in chains. Middle-class white kids decided to aid their cause. Some were killed in the attempt and songs were written to record that part of history. Queens College student Paul Simon, a short-haired fraternity leader, emerged with "He Was My Brother," about the Freedom Riders. In "Michael, Andrew, and James" Richard Fariña wrote of Schwerner, Chaney, and Goodman, the three who were found buried down South in a river of blood. Eric Andersen, a Hobart dropout, gave us perhaps the classic song of the protest movement, "Thirsty Boots," concerning a peace marcher resting on the side of the road before resuming an incredible uphill march.

Most of the generation had never been anywhere near that road. The closest thing to protesting occurred when they stomped and screamed when one of their favorite folksingers failed to return for an encore. The last time the generation identified with blacks was back in the heyday of rhythm and blues. But now, put in the outcast minority role because of political opinions, choice of drug, and scruffy looks, for the first time they could understand the subtle (and not so subtle) workings of prejudice. The black man was considered by them a brother. How the black man considered *them* is another matter.

Finally the words, the songs, the messages all began to sink in and create a consciousness; a group feeling headed by the folksingers against the pagan world outside. This consciousness was shaped at marches and rallies and forged into something solid at Newport and Philadelphia folk festivals where people, camped out on the beaches, united by common values and the dope-sweet night, drew strength from each other; strength to be tested back home among the unenlightened.

This original togetherness developed in the mid-sixties would eventually lead to the communal West Coast Summer Of Love and acid dream, which was led, in turn, by the new rock groups.

"I Like To Sleep Late In The Morning," by David Blue, 1964

Flunking out of school could be accepted, even though your parents might be severely disappointed. But leaving school while you were passing was something very different, an act of defiance almost. Nobody left school! It was even hard to explain this decision to friends, for although friends might secretly envy the dropout, on the surface they could not afford to let it show—even to themselves—lest they begin to question what *they* were doing in school. Once questions like that were permitted to enter everyday conversation, there could be no controlling the consequences—the whole plan could go out the window along with the book of rules. And so, just as dope became a dividing line, so did the issue of staying in school or dropping out. And since dropping out usually meant confronting the draft, the heaviness of the move could not be contested.

If the dropout merely wanted out of school in order to begin working, his status in the group was not really hurt. But if his dropping out was more of a political nature, for instance, to live in the Village, smoke dope, and protest the war, then his old friends generally wanted no part of him. He was written off as a cop-out, unable to compete in the marketplace of the real world, a dreamer trying to justify his laziness with slogans.

Which, of course, was not a thought unknown to the dropout himself, if he thought at all. Perhaps he was the victim of some great delusion and not a hero as he was led to believe. Not a pioneer, but a dupe, indulging himself while the rest of the world sped by laughing. Was there really anything at stake? The folk songs of the day outlined what seemed to be a new way of living, unprogrammed, undefined, revolutionary, expanding the mind and body, liberated from old-fashioned morality. But who could really live that way except the folksingers themselves . . . for whom it was a career.

So the dropout attended the marches; went to Newport and Philadelphia in search of more than just his folk-music dreamgirl; drew spiritual comfort from literature, from the songs, and from the growing numbers in the movement. But on the outside the war continued, and friends, once college freshmen, approached graduation. It was easy at such times to long for the old rules, the comforts of home. But harder still would be to admit defeat, give up the dream.

As a sidelight, sleeping until noon became a standard part of the dropout schedule. Since the early dropouts were few and far between and usually didn't know each other, there was nothing like sleeping until noon to kill an otherwise boring and uneventful day.

"Michael, Row The Boat Ashore," by D. Fisher, 1961

Folk music as showcased on the charts had been with us since 1959. The Kingston Trio had hit the top with "Tom Dooley"; Harry Belafonte sang of "Mary Ann," for a short while initiating a calypso craze; the Brothers Four gave us "Greenfields"; and Peter, Paul, and Mary brought Bob Dylan to the attention of the masses. The Highwaymen sang "Michael, Row The Boat Ashore" and made it the big folk hit of 1961.

On college campuses everywhere in the early sixties foursomes made up of identically straw-hatted crooners, cleancut in matching checkered shirts and white socks (one of them played banjo; one of them sang soprano) burst from the woodwork complete with repertoires ranging from "The Sloop John B." to "If I Had A Hammer" to "John Henry"—ballads which had nothing to do with what was going on just down the street. (Although my own favorite at the time, The Chad Mitchell Trio, did sing pungent topical protest . . . and eventually produced John Denver . . . I don't hold that against them.)

Through the courtesy of the "Hootenanny" show on national television, groups like the New Christy Minstrels and Young Americans for Mediocrity spread a folk image across the land embodied by the concept of togetherness. This togetherness included parents, too—sing-along with mom and dad—and was quickly taken into the mainstream of American life. This clean image of fireside folksinging, however, the camp-counselor-good-kid-college-youth (how come you never hear about the *good* teen-agers—because they never *do* anything), was nowhere near what real contemporary writing was all about.

The goody-goody folksingers (and their prematurely mature followers) never saw beyond their ivory towers into the street. One of the few to escape the stigma was Peter, Paul, and Mary. In fact, Peter Yarrow's "The Great Mandalla" stands as one of the best works of the era. Much later, even parents would suspect that there was something happening . . . and it had nothing to do with them.

PHIL OCHS

For a long period of time in Greenwich Village, Phil Ochs served as a sort of town crier. Each month at the Sunday Songwriters Workshop held at the Village Gate, crowds of expectant fans lined up to wait for another batch of Ochs' originals, and each month a new edition of instant current events analysis in song form would issue from him. The first and foremost of our protest singers and a fixture at rallies, marches, conventions, and all significant social happenings of the entire decade, Phil Ochs carved a place for himself with his seemingly endless series of epic songs—complicated, stirring, and deftly rhymed.

Today, looking back at his songs, we can see some of the same problems still facing us. They are a grim reminder of what the sixties in this country were all about and at the same time point up the changing sensibilities of the seventies. Certainly, among all the new songwriters, there is no new Phil Ochs to be found, unless of course it is the old Phil Ochs, who periodically shows signs of staging a verbal return to the fields of battle.

The interview with the verbose Mr. Ochs took place in the offices of A&M Records in New York City.

"I didn't even think about being a writer, it didn't cross my mind until about 1960. I was down in Florida and I was arrested for vagrancy. I spent fifteen days in jail and somewhere during the course of those fifteen days I decided to become a writer. My primary thought was journalism. I'd been to college for two years and I didn't have a major, so in a flash I decided —I'll be a writer, and I'll major in journalism.

"This was the period when folk music was on the rise, when John Kennedy had just come in and Fidel Castro had just come in. Those forces just sort of took me over. I mean Kennedy got me superficially interested in politics, and Castro got me into serious politics, socialism, and anti-imperialism. He became the teacher of anti-imperialism of that time period by surviving. And at the same time I started writing songs—I'll never know why, but out they came.

"There were a couple of little ditties I wrote in jail, but they aren't anything. The first regular song was called, 'The Ballad Of The Cuban Invasion.' Those early songs were all sort of political—about Freedom Riders, Billy Sol Estes, the AMA. They just came out, no effort, no strain, absolutely no training, just bang-o—songs—one after another, and it lasted from 1961 to 1970.

"At school my roommate was Jim Glover of Jim and Jean. He gave me a few guitar chords and that week I wrote a song. It was the impulse of journalism—you know, you've got to get that story in. The infatuation with folk music and fifties rock, the newness of politics . . . all fused in my first songs. In school I had my own paper called *The Word,* which was a very radical paper, which is where I saw the fundamental weakness of journalism. I had an editorial saying, at the peak of the anti-Castro hysteria, that Fidel Castro is perhaps the greatest man that this century has produced in the Western Hemisphere. And this caused a giant storm, and I was taken off political stories in the local newspaper. So I saw the way bureaucracy censors people. At the same time I went to a journalism fraternity meeting where I saw the same people that sacked me swearing an oath of allegience to Truth. I had one of my first impulses to murder, which I still haven't lost.

"I would sing the songs for Jim right away. I sang with him for six months in a group called the Sundowners. Sort of Bud and Travis stuff, early Seals and Crofts. He loved the songs. After we both quit school we split up. I got a job in a club called Farrager's in Cleveland, which was good training, considering that I'd only been playing a half a year. To go public with new songs at a point when new songs weren't fashionable, before Dylan had entered the scene, was a very tough experience. So I was opening act to a lot of really good people like Judy Henske, the Smothers Brothers. Bob Gibson was a big influence on me musically. So I quickly gained the professionalism onstage. I was thrown to the wolves when I came out. I did my early political songs and a couple of, say, Kingston Trio things thrown in."

From there Phil journeyed east.

"Everybody said go to New York and I figured, well New York is the tiger's den, I can't go up against those pros. But I went to New York and right away I met Dylan and I said, 'Oh my God, this is the guy!' As soon as I heard him sing his first song I flipped out. And of course there were also a good ten or fifteen other people around who wrote songs. At that time songwriting was still unfashionable—I mean it was still the euphoria of ethnic folk or commercial folk. Folk being defined by age, songwriting being defined as pretense. You can't write a folk song, that argument. You can't use it for propaganda. You can't use folk music for politics was also a side argument. The breakthrough was Newport sixty-three with the Freedom Singers, Dylan, Baez, the songwriter's workshop, where it suddenly became the thing. It moved from the background into the foreground in just one weekend.

"After that I got an album out and I was completely prolific; I was writing all the time. Quickly followed by another album, followed by a concert.

"My thought throughout this whole time period was, all right, here we have the form of a song, how important can a song be? Can it rival a play? Can it rival a movie? Can it make a statement that's as deep as a book? And by making a simple point can it reach more people than a book ever can? That was always in the back of my mind. And I was completely political, as I still am, and I thought, being a socialist, what political effect can these songs have? I saw it with my own eyes; I sang the songs, they came through me, and I saw they had a political effect on the audience.

"Like I was writing about Vietnam in 1962, way before the first anti-war marches. I was writing about it at a point where the media were really full of shit, where they were just turning the other way as Vietnam was being built. It was clear to me and some others—I. F. Stone—but *The New York Times,* CBS, Walter Cronkite, and all those other so-called progressive forces chose to look the other way for several years before they decided it had gone too far. But it had already gone too far back then. People had seen the handwriting on the wall.

"So my songs served that function. Everything I wrote was on instinct. There was some sort of psychic force at work in those songs and I don't know what it was. It's a strange way of giving birth; ideas giving birth in song form. And when the songs came they came fast. I don't think I ever spent more than two hours on any one song. Even 'Crucifixion' was done in two hours.

"That period in the Village was incredibly exciting, super-euphoric. There was total creativity on the part of a great number of individuals that laid the bedrock for the next ten years. But everything goes in cycles, everything has a life span and I guess this life span just ran out. Even though everyone from that period has sort of petered out, the important thing to bear in mind in terms of a whole life is, I mean you take a whole life, whether it's ten years or sixty years and say, what has this person done, what has he accomplished, if anything? He's now dead, what has he left behind him of value? And I think the people who made that contribution in the sixties can rest on that.

"Hopefully some will continue on, like Joni Mitchell is doing. But if they don't—like I mean Tim Hardin has made a major contribution and it doesn't matter if Tim Hardin ever leaves his house again, he's already done it. The big question mark is, where is the new generation? We're all waiting for them. But for whatever reasons they're not coming out yet. Jackson Browne, John Prine, Bruce Springsteen, Steve Goodman, they're all—I hate to be so crass—but they're all interesting possibilities. Nobody's gone over the line yet. You know, like that Joni Mitchell song, 'Carey,' I mean you can tell she went over the line with that. She left her ego behind and got into a fabulous song . . . and you can hear it in her songwriting, the sense of liberation she achieves. I don't think these other people have done it yet. They're all writing pleasant tunes, nice little words, but they're all derivative. To be considered a serious artist you've got to break new ground, to have people say '*he* did that, *she* did this' and it opens up and you can tell when it opens up; you can just feel it happen.

"I mean Joni Mitchell is the only one who seems to be developing like a true artist, like a painter or a sculptor, with serious long-range stuff, constant growth, constant activity, and I really admire her for that. Plus she's developing a fabulous singing style, also improving all the time. It's wonderful to see somebody who's able to grow in difficult times—God bless her.

"As far as music goes today I think we're in kind of a stalemate. Country music is probably in the forefront of all writing at the moment. Merle Haggard, Charlie Rich, Dolly Parton, Jerry Lee Lewis, these are people whom I think are making the best music. I think it's very interesting that they've been able to survive and continue creating. I mean Jerry Lee Lewis is getting close to forty, and still he's putting out record after record.

"The old-time songwriters were more trained. The sixties were very instinctual and untrained and that's what's showing now, the lack of discipline and training as inspiration runs out. I mean a lot of these people are laymen; it was basically a layman's revolution. These people don't know much more about music than the average guy on the street.

"For me songwriting was easy from 1961 to 1966 and then it got more and more difficult. It could be alcohol; it could be the deterioration of the politics I was involved in. It could be a general deterioration of the country. Basically, me and the country were deteriorating simultaneously and that's probably why it stopped coming. Part of the problem was that there was never any pattern to my writing. The point of discipline is to create your own pattern so you can write, and I haven't done that. I always make plans to do that—I'm now thirty-three and I may or may not succeed. But ever since the late sixties that's constantly on my mind—discipline, training, get it together, clean up your act. I haven't been able to do it yet, but the impulse is as strong as ever. To my dying day I'll always think about the next possible song, even if it's twenty years from now. I'll never make the conscious decision to stop writing.

"But getting back to music today, I consider rock music basically dead, uninteresting, boring, repetitious, too loud, egomaniacal, ludicrous, and totally beside the point, and I can't be too strong about that. To me there's no point in having Ringo Starr put out 'You're Sixteen' with a great production job in back of him—which is not a tenth as good as Johnny Burnette's original. There's no point to it in terms of the importance of music."

In the seventies Phil Ochs has returned to his first interest, journalism.

"In 1973 I wrote six articles on weird little subjects, some Nixon political stuff, predicting the fall of Agnew and the fall of Nixon—that they both had to go, period. I did an article on Bruce Lee, the Chinese–American actor that died this year; an article on Mike Mazurky, an American character actor and wrestler; an article on Tom Reddin, police chief running for mayor in Los Angeles.

"The articles came out the same way. It was very painful to start it, but once I got started it flowed smoothly, and after I got done I was very happy with it. The next article would start out just as hard. My mind is like an engine in the middle of winter, it just won't start . . . then once in a while it catches on. I'm sure that's the story of my life. Things come in a flash, like the way I wrote songs. The same impulse that said there's a great song here would say there's a great story here.

"Also I've been traveling a lot. I go to a different country every year. In 1971 I went to South America, in 1972 I went to Australia and New Zealand and Southeast Asia. This year I went to Africa for three months. In Africa I wrote two songs. One side was translated into Swahili, the other into Lingala. The Swahili song concerns the life of the herdsman, the guy you see at the African roadside standing with a spear with the cows. The other is sort of a general freedom song based on a traditional melody."

I asked Phil if criticism had any affect on him.

"If I liked a song I had total confidence in it and it doesn't matter if people said it's a great song or a lousy song. Hysterical praise or hysterical attacks didn't affect me at all. It's always been between me and my songs, not about the critics, not about the public, not about sales or anything else. 'Crucifixion,' 'Changes,' 'I Ain't Marchin' Anymore,' 'There But For Fortune,' and a couple of songs I liked that the general public didn't, such as 'I've Had Her,' 'Bach, Beethoven, Mozart, and Me,' are my personal favorites.

"It's always been a question of will it stand the test of time? That was always one of the things in the very early days, before Dylan left politics, when he and I were writing political songs. There were two attacks: You can't write folk music, and you can't use folk music for propaganda. Besides it's topical and it'll be meaningless two years from then. And so to sing 'Small Circle Of Friends,' seven years later and still get the same response, gives the lie to that attack. Whether the audience is hearing it for the first or the fifteenth time it still holds up. It could be nostalgia for some people, but on the other hand, there's some essential truth locked up in that song, and it's locked up to a thirteen-year-old kid that hears it today for the first time. He responds to it because the truth is there. In a way it's more there than ever, than even when I wrote it.

"I'd just like to add that I never had anything against Dylan when he stopped writing political songs. In that controversy I was always completely on his side. The thing that's important about a writer is whether or not he's writing good stuff. It's not important if he's writing politics, leftwing, rightwing, or anything. Is it good, is it great, does it work? When Dylan made the switch I said he's writing as good or better. And when he made his *Highway 61* album I said, this is it, his apex; it's fantastic. But after his hiatus, when he came back and made his recent albums, at that point I couldn't go along with Dylan, because he'd reached his heights, and I couldn't accept what I considered lightweight stuff.

"But if you're writing a book on song lyrics I'd make a statement that Dylan was by far the best song lyricist that ever lived, and probably ever will live. He's in a class by himself."

I asked Phil where he was when rock 'n' roll broke out.

"I was going to military school in Virginia. I had no idea what I was going to be. I wasn't political; I wasn't musical. I was just an American nebbish, being formed by societal forces, completely captivated by movies, the whole James Dean–Marlon Brando trip. I was about sixteen. My brother was heavy into rhythm and blues. I was into country and western music. I memorized all those songs, my music teacher being the radio. There was Webb Pierce, Ray Price, Johnny Cash, Faron Young. And then I really fell for the Elvis image.

"I recently came to the conclusion that Colonel Parker knows more about organizing America than Angela Davis or SDS. He understands the American mentality. In terms of changes in America you have to reach the working class, and to me Elvis Presley, in retrospect, is like a giant commercialization of the working class singer, also a true integrationist in terms of bringing black music and country music together, which is why his strength is so long-lasting. His gold suit was Parker's idea of the super-gross carnival treatment, a cheap icon of all America has to offer.

"That was part of the idea behind my *Greatest Hits* album, an idea which has yet to be consummated. I had another insight about it when I saw the truckers strike blocking the highways. The whole way they dealt with the truckers was to play them that country music. There are waves of restlessness sweeping through those kinds of people, which is why they find themselves in the awkward situation of being like the students they were hating five years ago. My most recent album *Gunfight at Carnegie Hall* is the companion piece to *Greatest Hits*. If you listen to both together, the whole thing makes sense, but neither one alone is quite complete."

Briefly, *Gunfight at Carnegie Hall* is a live album of a concert at which Phil Ochs appeared in a gold suit, encountering massive resistance from his audience.

"*Gunfight* is an explanation of why the gold suit. *Greatest Hits* was the germinal idea of that thing, which is fifties rock, primeval rock, done with lyrics that are addressed to real problems. The key songs would be 'My Kingdom For A Car,' or 'Gas Station Woman.' These songs were both in the direction

I wanted to head in that I was stymied by, but that I would hope to get back to. I mean 'Gas Station Woman' could be sung easily by Ray Price. 'Kingdom For A Car' could be done by Jerry Lee Lewis.

"I happened to meet Jack Clement, who produced all the Jerry Lee hits and is a Nashville shitkicker, and I laid a copy of *Greatest Hits* on him in Hollywood. He went back to Nashville and I was lying in bed in Hollywood and at three o'clock in the morning the phone rings and it's Jack Clement calling from Nashville. He says, 'Phil, I've been sitting here all night playing "My Kingdom For A Car." When I met you I had no idea you knew about this kind of stuff.' He talked for two hours and I don't know what he said, but he raved about the song and then he hung up.

"So, in other words, it contacted. It didn't contact with the public, but the record was worth doing just for the Jack Clement phone call. I was on the right road; I just haven't followed it up. But I'm still interested in that train of thought.

I asked him if there was a market on the top hundred for Phil Ochs' songs.

"I'm amazed that 'Changes' wasn't a hit. We've got about twenty recordings on it. Done by Roberta Flack or Anne Murray I'm sure it would be a number one song. 'There But For Fortune' was a hit, but it certainly wasn't written as one. Joan Baez just happened to pick it up and it caught on. I think 'Flower Lady' could catch at any time with the right group. At one time the Byrds were going to do it—that's another one of my disappointments. I think if they had done it, it could have been a hit.

"My favorite recording of one of my songs in Anita Bryant doing 'Power and Glory' on her patriotic record—it's unbelievable. She has an album out called *Mine Eyes Have Seen The Glory*—it's straight patriotic stuff. She does a version of 'Power and Glory' on it that's unbelievable, I mean really incredible. I think if a song has enough meaning it can survive anything."

BUFFY SAINTE-MARIE

Buffy came to prominence during the folk era, hoisted to underground approval on the virtue of her classic "Universal Soldier" and her first album of unique and disturbing songs, entitled *It's My Way*. Before long she was a Greenwich Village fixture, playing on bills with Phil Ochs, Eric Andersen, and Tom Paxton. She and Joni Mitchell were certainly the pioneering female songwriters of the decade.

Although some of her most deeply felt creations have related to her Cree Indian background ("Now That The Buffalo's Gone"), she has written of many other experiences—battles with drugs ("Cod'ine"), women's protest ("Babe In Arms"), personal freedom ("It's My Way"), and a new definition of romantic love ("Until It's Time For You To Go").

Back on the concert circuit in the seventies, after much time spent abroad, Buffy is now writing and singing . . . rock 'n' roll!

A natural artist and intuitive poet, Buffy Sainte-Marie is articulate as well as passionate on the subject of writing. The interview took place at a restaurant in Greenwich Village.

"I've always been an inventor and a creator of my own world, partly because of unavoidable isolation and partly because of solitude not imposed so much as chosen. I've always enjoyed being by myself and have also fallen into that kind of situation from the time when I was growing up to now, being on the road. The pattern of my life seems to be that I'm alone a lot.

"I don't sit down with a pencil and paper and write poems and songs and stories, but I always have poetic ideas and music going on in my head. It's like a constant radio station of my own. I hear the music and the words at the same time and I

have to feel, in the case of a 'song' that they're just wedded together. I can't notate music very well, so I have to remember things. If it's exciting enough for me to remember it, then it's exciting enough to share with people.

"It's something I'm able to do. It's totally a gift. It's not something I did because I was a singer and I needed some songs. I've always been able to do it and I've always appreciated it. I swear it saved my life a number of times because I've felt down, ill, unable to cope with things, especially when I was in high school; and the music, I don't understand it at all, but it's healed me on a number of occasions. And I've found that it's healed other people too.

"I can't force it. People have asked me to write movie scores and toothpaste commercials, things that I could really make a lot of money with—and I would love to divert that money toward some things that I would like to see done—but I'm really not very confident about being able to write on a schedule. I probably could do it if they caught me on the right day, but I couldn't promise I'd have a song by next Thursday at four P.M. I once wrote a whole series of commercials for Jell-O. All of a sudden I got these commercials for Jell-O in my head. Visuals and everything. But I never sent them in. It's like dreaming a dream. Sometimes the music will keep me up at night. It's just there and if it wants to play with me and I don't get up, it keeps me awake.

"When I say 'play' I mean *play,* because music for me is play no matter how serious it is, because I've never been forced to take lessons, I've never been forced to write, I've never been trained to write. It started out maybe just being a pastime, an escape from homework, an escape from doing things the way everybody wanted me to do them, which I never did very well . . . and then I found I could invent my own music, keep myself company with it, express myself with it, but most of all *play* with it.

"In growing, I've never felt obligated to consistency in any

form, including my own personality. A lot of people are created by their parents. I was adopted, which automatically gave
me a sense of distance. The next personality people develop is
usually as a result of a lover, so they realize they can be something else other than what their parents created, what their
high-school playmates created. All of a sudden they have two
personalities available to them. The Women's Movement has
shown a lot of women that there's a third personality—'myself,
I, the woman.' I found that out so, so long ago, and I've found
that not only are those three personalities available to me, but
there are forty or fifty or a hundred others. There's something
new everyday, and I write from whatever feeling I'm getting
within myself.

"If I'm happy, that's what I share. If a song has come to me
and brought me up, that's what I'll give to people. If a song
is about things that I've seen, like 'Universal Soldier' or 'Now
That The Buffalo's Gone,' I'll write that too. Those are really
college student songs. They're not like 'Sweet Little Vera,' they
can't reach everybody. A thirteen-year-old or someone who's
mentally retarded can't know what 'Universal Soldier' is about.
'Sweet Little Vera' he can feel, it's emotional, it brings him up
. . . because it's a feel-good song.

"My songs are collectively reflective of my entire personality,
and I'm very varied. 'Until It's Time For You To Go' is nothing like 'Universal Soldier' which is nothing like 'Sweet Little
Vera' which is nothing like 'Piney Wood Hills.' I'm not with
one person all the time and I don't write one kind of song. If
someone were to say they didn't think I should sing this or that
because I sang something else that they liked better and they
only think I should write one kind of song, it would just make
me laugh."

I asked Buffy what she meant by a college student song.

"A college kind of song would be like 'My Country Tis of
Thy People You're Dying,' you know, it's a condensation of
Native American [Indian] history. It's six minutes to make up

for the total lack of candor and truth and information available to the American people about Indians. 'Universal Soldier,' 'Suffer The Little Children,' they're high protein lectures is what they are. I wanted 'Universal Soldier' to do what it did. I wanted it to get people out of their classrooms and onto their feet. But certain things I have to say are pitched at too high a level to bring any lasting benefit to as many people as I would like to bring it to. If I have something of myself that gets me off, that's brought me through hard times and that refreshes and nourishes me, what good does it do if I'm not smart enough to get it to the people? And I don't mean only the people who are like me, I mean all the people. That's communication. There's no sense being a closet genius. It doesn't do me any good to keep the medicine in the bottle."

What other types of songs does she write?

"I have more love songs than anything else I think. I have fifty or sixty love songs I haven't recorded. There are intellectual songs, there are rock 'n' roll songs, and then there's another kind of song like 'Starboy' which is really kind of intimate poetry. The only artist I know who does this kind of song in about the same way is Joni Mitchell—she does that real well. There are light kind of story-telling songs, like 'Poor Man's Daughter' and there are country songs. I write a lot of songs in Cree that I only sing to Indian people. But 'Native North American Child,' 'Generation,' and 'He's An Indian Cowboy At The Rodeo' have been giant hits everywhere except in America. America is not ready yet to look at the American Indian except as a victim. That's the only way anyone here wants to see him.

"I never write the same song twice, but some songs go in generations. 'Moratorium' is not 'Universal Soldier' but it's like 'son of.' I mean, five lears later 'Universal Soldier' is still true, but it hasn't said enough and I have to write another song because that's what's in my head.

"I also write what I call healing songs. I guess they're on the same level as religious songs, but they're not gospel kind of religious songs; they're the kind of song you'd sing to a person who really needed them. They're medicine songs. Some of them are in French, some in Cree, some in English, some in Hawaiian. Some don't have words at all, only sounds; they're in Human. I haven't recorded them, but I have sung them in a lot of instances.

"Let me tell you something about American audiences. They mostly want to hear things that sound like they've heard them before. In other parts of the world that's not necessarily so. My songs are always at least two years ahead of their time. For two years I was criticized for writing 'Universal Soldier.' For two years I couldn't sing 'Now That The Buffalo's Gone' on television. Two years after I'd written it they finally let me sing it. Everybody wanted to be an Indian, right? But they wouldn't let me sing 'My Country Tis Of Thy People You're Dying' because it was too strong. Two years went by, now that's all they want me to sing.

"I wrote 'Until It's Time For You To Go' and the folkies called me a sellout. I wore sparkles on my clothes and tight satiny dresses and high heels because that's the way I felt and it was the wrong way to feel at the Newport Folk Festival because it wasn't what Joanie and Bobby were wearing. I mean, for me music in ninety-nine percent of my life. I've sold out everything else. I've sold out my heart. I've sold out my head. I've sold out my body. I've sold out everything from my health to any lover I've ever had. When it's time to get on that airplane that's it. It's partly because I'm drawn as a performer and partly because I'm pushed by the music. I love being a performer. I think it's a noble profession."

Buffy explained her attitude about which songs she chooses to perform in public.

"I'm both an artist and a professional. The artist in me has great respect for the professional side. I have lots of songs I don't sing to other people. It's not a matter of commercialism so much as communication. Communication is my art. What I choose of my songs to get across to the people is conditioned by two things: it's usually the middle ground between one, where I'm at; and two, where whoever I want to reach is at . . . cause it doesn't do enough good to put out an entire album of songs that only four people in the world are going to understand. The songs I select to perform are determined by what I want to do that night, but for the most part now, in 1974, I'm trying to fill in a gap that has had to do with who I am in relation to the crowd that used to come and see me in the Village. Due to circumstances beyond my control people have not been exposed to all the feelings that I want to share, let alone all the ideas that I have, that my head sent me in terms of songs that I'm willing to share and able to share on a lot of different levels. I feel I have an obligation to an audience, and I don't sing just for college students or just to Indians or just for women or just for rock 'n' roll lovers. I know for a fact that because the audience reaches me I'm going to reach them. It's an interaction between me and my life and between me and the audience."

Buffy was not always a performer, although she always played music. Until she got to college she was extremely shy.

"While I was in college my shyness kind of melted day by day through getting to know a lot of people. I wasn't in the high school situation of a small community; I went to a huge school, University of Massachusetts, and I was with new people all the time. I felt I didn't have to be any one special way.

"So I used to just sing in the dorm, just my own songs, for one or two friends. And I found that they really were feeling exceptionally good by the time I finished singing. I really began developing it as a kind of healing art for my friends. I never thought I'd wind up in the razzle dazzle of show business.

"This songwriting stuff was just the same thing that was going on when I was supposed to be studying my math in high school. Or when I was supposed to be saying the right thing at the right time in the girls' lavatory. I mean, I thought I was crazy for a long time. I was just miserable in high school because I always had this music in my head and I didn't *want* to go to school. I just wanted to stay home and play the piano, even if I could only play in one key, even if I couldn't read music and flunked music class all the time.

"So I was finally able, within my own personality, to share what was already going on in my head. I didn't write songs in order to please people, but I began exhibiting what I was already digging to do, and able to do, for myself. I began sharing the music with other people."

Those who have followed Buffy from album to album might be surprised to learn who her first influence was.

"The first musician who really flashed me was Elvis Presley. It was for personality, it was for sex, it was because of music, it was because of chord changes. I mean, there was never a boy like that in my home town! That got me moving and I mean it, and it's affected me all through my travels and my performances."

The last thing we talked about was Buffy's ensemble.

"Let me tell you something about being a writer and having a band at your disposal. It could be devastating unless you have very generous musicians. As a writer it enables me to be like five writers at once. In other words, when I go in to record a song, it's not only the words and the melody that makes it me, it's the whole arrangement.

"I'll play the song once on the piano and the piano player will watch what I do, then he'll play the same kind of runs that I do. Then I'll play it on guitar and the same thing happens. So there's me playing the piano and me playing the guitar and I'm also free to sing. The drummer will put down my licks. The bass player will look at the patterns that I'm doing. And then when we're playing it all together they'll add their own creativity and skill to the song, but basing the arrangement on my ideas. It will take probably a half an hour to record the song. It's lightning fast and it's always fresh, but it takes an extraordinary combination of musicians to build the song without destroying it.

"It's a new high every time. I can't tell you how thrilling the whole song receiving-writing-performing process is. If a song comes into my head it's a high. The first time you play it on guitar it's another high, a different high. Then I play it on piano. Then you play it for someone for the first time and you see it react on them. It's like an entire growing up process. You learn that you have a body, then you learn that you can feel your body, then you learn you can do incredible things by feeling your body. Then you learn you can give your body to somebody else and let them feel it. It's the same thing. I can give a song to the musicians and I can feel what each person does with each song each night, how they change it, how they manipulate it.

"I'm a professional performer but not a professional song-writer. Composing is just a question of allowing the music to come to me and accepting the music. You don't get to judge the music that comes into your head (or I know I don't!). I don't judge it; I just accept it and then I filter it for an audience. It's the performer in me that filters it for an audience. I'm not going to sing something for somebody that I think is just going to bore them. As a performer I'd feel like a robber if I did that. But as a writer, I just write whatever comes into my head.

"The only thing wrong with traveling around and being on the run is there's just not enough music on the road. Instead of doing interviews like this I'd much rather, excuse me, be back at my place playing the piano and rehearsing with the band. I'd rather be doing that than anything else in the world."

PART
THREE

England Swings:
1964–1965

(Invasion of the Allies)

"Can't Buy Me Love," by Lennon and McCartney, 1964

The arrival of the Beatles on these shores in the early part of 1964 caused many a barber to go prematurely gray. Hair past the collar! Hair covering the ears! Foreheads disappearing under layers and layers of hair! Long after a list of their achievements have been read into the holy scroll and maybe forgotten, the memory of what the Beatles did to hair styles will linger in the minds of crewcut mothers and fathers everywhere, from Utica, New York, to Muskogee, Oklahoma. In fact, if one had to sum up the generation gap in a word or less, he would be hard pressed to come up with a better choice than . . . hair.

We had a guy in my neighborhood about this time, 1964, this kid with the longest hair I'd ever seen on a guy. Every once in a while late at night I'd spot him heading into the candy store or emerging from the drugstore with a package tucked secretly under his arm. An original freak with hair showering over his shoulders. It looked like he hadn't cut it for a year or more. A year or more!

You have to understand that until this point men and boys had been virtual prisoners of the barber chair . . . that once-a-month "just a little off the sides, Sal," ritual. Barbers were known to be in league with Indians, or at least to have some sort of deal with them to sell our locks by the pound on the black market. No matter how much coaching you might give them beforehand, "Could you leave it long in the back, Tony?" "Sure, Ace." *Whomp! Zwock!* All haircuts ended up the same, with that draftee crop and a soaking down with Vitalis . . . plus the obligatory pompadour! We were a generation of Bonny Prince Charleys.

And forget about sideburns! Prior to 1964 the only persons with sideburns were pimps, bookies, known rapists, public enemies, hoods, mechanics, or Southerners. And since barbers at that time were among those public figures considered authorities (along with teachers, doctors, dentists, policemen, shopkeepers, etc.) it was upon their good opinion that your well-being depended. Ask a barber to let your sideburns grow, before 1964, and you were just about through in the neighborhood.

Which brings me back to my original freak. Everyone knew who this guy was and referred to him as "the kid with the hair" but no one seemed to know him personally. What was he like? Did he go to school? Was he interested in sports? Maybe he smoked dope. (Did smoking dope have some sort of effect on the hair?) Everyone was somewhat afraid to approach him.

As the sixties progressed hair became a symbol, a definition, a label of identity, a source of pride. People were thrown out of school over the excessive length of their hair. Homes were broken up because a father couldn't tell his son from his daughter. Sideburned youths were drummed from the Boy Scouts. Clean-up hitters banished from the Little League for wearing long hair. Employment agencies wouldn't send a long-haired applicant on any decent job interviews. People across from longhairs on the subway would look askance. The mother of your blind date, if you had shaggy locks, would ask you if your parents were still living. Your blind date herself would edge away from you in the movie theater. In the South Peter Fonda and Dennis Hopper were shot in the back.

Blame it on the Beatles!

With the unprecedented flurry of furry-haired rock groups in the mid-sixties, long hair became synonymous with loud music, depravity, homosexual tendencies, and communist leanings. From one freak per neighborhood (the true heroes of our time!) the ratio soon increased to one per block, and then two (who quickly became friends). By 1966 the count had risen to approximately one per family—your crazy cousin Kevin, who used to belch aloud in the third grade.

And then beards! Goatees! Moustaches! Sideburns connected to moustaches. Moustaches connected to goatees. Ponytails returned, this time for men! Long hair served as an admission ticket to an exclusive order of being. You nodded when another freak walked by, even if you lived in New York City. One freak would *always* stop his car for another, even if the other wasn't looking for a ride.

Of course, by 1968 or so, long hair became the standard for the Young Modern, the adman, school teacher, furniture salesman—the jock down the block even had hair bunching out of his baseball cap! At last fathers gave in and liberated their own muttonchops. By then hair had run its course politically. Hair had been to the top of the charts ("Hair," by the Cowsills), had been a hit on Broadway (*Hair!* lyrics by Rado and Ragni). When every rube on the street had long hair, it was impossible to spot the authentic pioneer from the bandwagon groupies.

By the turn of the decade, in scattered sectors, the odd skinhead could be seen wandering dead-end streets, in search of a friend.

"I Feel Fine," by Lennon and McCartney, 1964
As a musical entity the Beatles were obsessed with love. Of the eleven songs which made the Billboard Top Ten under the banner of the Beatles in 1964, ten of them dealt directly with love, and the eleventh was not their own composition.

"I Want To Hold Your Hand"—primitive contact, bursting adolescent feelings of love; "She Loves You"—relaying the good news that your girl friend still cares; "Please Please Me"—demanding equal love rights; "Can't Buy Me Love"—the pricelessness of the product; "Do You Want To Know A Secret"—*guess* what the secret is (you guessed it); "Love Me Do"—more youthful gurglings on the subject; "P.S. I Love You"—as if we didn't know; "Hard Day's Night"—coming home to the woman he loves; "She's A Woman"—who knows how to love her man; "I Feel Fine"—and no wonder!

If you need further proof of their illness, just look at the only song they gave to another group to make into a hit—"A World Without Love," by Peter and Gordon, written by John and Paul, which went in part, "I don't care what they say I can't stay in a world without love." That was really telling it like it was! Those chaps couldn't bear even the possibility, so they had to let someone else record those words—and the song, like the others, hit number one in the country.

In 1964 a lot of rock 'n' roll fans didn't like the thought of a world without love either. They were a generation crushed by outside events, the Kennedy assassination and its grissly aftermath being the primary one. The radical youth had already pitched their tents in the protest camp. For the rest, rock 'n' roll was the only reality; and Marty Robbins had left them in "El Paso," "Big Bad John" had perished in the mines, and "Teen Angel" was four years gone.

So the emergence of four really hip guys, dressed to the teeth (unlike the ragged folksingers), funny cats, sharp talkers, with this fine long hair . . . who sang about love, nothing but love. . . . Love, love, love. . . . All day and all night love oh love . . . without ceasing . . . for a year . . . was a blessing. The Beatles single-handedly (or is it eight-handedly?) made it hip for great masses of kids to smile again.

Every Lennon and McCartney song, one after another, went zinging straight to that place where all hit records go. Zing! Zing! Beyond a matter of formula, John and Paul *were* pop music from the instant they came on the American scene. We'd never heard their like before. Elvis didn't really write his own songs, and besides, he'd already sold out to Hollywood. Even Neil Sedaka missed once in a while. But the Beatles hit the target every shot. Lennon and McCartney wrote so many instantly mesmerizing songs that the singles market was just not big enough to handle them. Instead of changing their pace, they wound up revolutionizing the album market and, in the process, changing the buying habits of a generation.

In 1964 the only people under thirty who bought albums were the folk music devotees, simply because their favorites by and large could not be heard on AM radio. Rock 'n' roll groups, on the other hand, tailor-made their product for the three-minute requirements of the AM band—the rock albums usually contained their hit record together with nine or ten B-sides (rejects). Therefore, kids bought the hit record and let the albums rot in the stacks where they belonged. But when the Beatles started coming out with albums which contained great sides not released as singles, well, the albums became a necessity of life. By this time allowances were hefty enough to support such a purchase and this was not lost on music-business magnates, who saw a market where it had not hitherto existed. Every act began beefing up their album product, using higher grade songs, not just filler. And the album market was born . . . because of the Beatles.

And then, the Beatles wrote all of their own material. Not only did this lead other creative teens into trying the same (writing rock 'n' roll songs, as opposed to composing the obscure editorials of folk protest music), but it also encouraged *industry moguls* to find and develop this talent. Surely if the Beatles could do it, they reasoned, there must be more gold in those hills.

This adventurous move of giving rock 'n' roll over to the people effectively loosened the Tin Pan Alley toehold on the Top Ten charts, and in the years to follow drove Tin Pan Alley to the poorhouse fair. (In the same way, Bob Dylan shifted the emphasis of folk music from the Childs' book of ballads to our own American creative folk poets.)

Not content with raising havoc in the music business, Lennon and McCartney next took on AM radio. AM radio had never had much room for album cuts, they were too long, weren't hitbound; but since the Beatles and competing album-oriented groups were recording five- or eleven-minute songs, a whole portion of the radio audience was being denied its music and losing interest in AM radio in the process. Every so often an AM station played an album cut, but it was not enough. And so free-form radio was created, carved from the classical music wasteland of the FM band, to deal with the exploding album scene. One thing led to another and soon groups counted on album sales to bring them fans rather than trying to create the hit single. For awhile the hit formula was discarded altogether in favor of experimentation in music and lyrics—with, of course, the Beatles leading the way.

And to wrap it up, the Beatles completely revamped the standard rock 'n' roll image, which up to that time had been not much removed from the standard American jock image—dumb, country, dull, a corporation stiff in baggy pants. The Beatles were openly bright (John Lennon had written a *book*). Also they were wiseacres, with long hair and no cuffs on their jeans. Many a fledgling wiseacre alone in his room could imagine himself up there in the spotlight whenever the Beatles took the stage . . . and wrote songs for this occasion . . . and packed themselves by the tens of thousands into arenas, halls, and ballparks across the country when the Beatles arrived on their first American tour.

"Under My Thumb," by Jagger and Richard, 1965

So America was waiting for the next thing and England gave it to her: Billy J. Kramer and the Dakotas, Gerry and the Pacemakers, Freddy and the Dreamers, Herman and the Hermits, Wayne Fontana and the Mindbenders, The Dave Clark Five (hooray for originality), The Zombies, The Kinks, Manfred Mann, The Animals, Peter and Gordon, Chad and Jeremy, Sybil and Richard.

During the years 1964 and 1965 English pop thoroughly dominated the American charts. Insipid carbon copies of each other, they snowed the locals here with their British accents, their Eton jackets, and their prep school smirks. They sang not of a particularly British experience either, but of an Americanized pop story we already knew and were sick of. Well, the Animals were a little hip, doing "House Of The Rising Sun," an old ballad which Dylan had done on his first album . . . and Herman may have been cuter than Frankie Avalon . . . and the Kinks were sort of daring with "All Day And All Of The Night," at least implying some healthy desires heretofore unheard on AM radio.

But the Rolling Stones made the English invasion worth it. The Stones were ugly and proud; they wore their bad looks like voodoo masks, threatening the onlooker with instant damnation if he dwelled on them too long. They were boys that mothers warned their daughters against—tough, seedy, vulgar, the antithesis of the clean Beatle image.

If the Beatles brought rock 'n' roll to new creative heights with their lively literary interest in love, the Stones succeeded in the other direction, offering the generation new lows in calculated vile and degenerate sexuality.

Mick Jagger was aware of the pent-up frustration and lust inside the average kid. He wrote of hours on the prowl for "Satisfaction," got put off by ritzy suburban girls like "Lady Jane," and dumb ones from the neighborhood like "Stupid Girl." When he found someone to hang out with he made his intentions known by suggesting "Let's Spend The Night Together." But he was something different for most girls, one who drove them to their "Nineteenth Nervous Breakdown," or the refuge of pills *a la* "Mother's Little Helper." Sure he was a sexist, but in fantasy we all were—and that's rock 'n' roll. After the childlike handholding ways of the Beatles, Jagger's approach certainly made a more viable fantasy, to say the least.

And so, just when parents were on the brink of accepting the Beatles as cute and tolerable (despite their long hair and snippy manner toward adults) along came the Rolling Stones to confirm that rock 'n' roll was still despicable, was still as full of lust as ever. For all the Beatles did in turning on a generation (paving the way for the full-scale love and peace and flowers movement later on), it was really the Rolling Stones who prevented rock 'n' roll from becoming merely updated pop music after all.

"My Generation," by Peter Townshend, 1965

The British rock invasion effectively switched world and tourist attention from MacDougal Street to Carnaby Street, from the emerging scruffy baby-hipster folk-music scene to the well-dressed, discrete decadence of the Mods and Rockers, opposing points in English low society.

Basically the Mods were into a lifestyle somewhat akin to the cruising syndrome prevalent on most American streets in the early sixties, except they were infinitely more committed to it. These were kids who religiously followed the fashion trends, inspected clothing labels and hung out in front of any modishly popular chain of clothing store, popping bennies and restlessly combing and recombing their hair. They danced, had feverish all-night parties . . . and were periodically attacked by the Rockers.

The Rockers were something like our bikers—brash, vicious, destructive types, who liked to bust up things—especially Mod pill parties. Nobody much cared for them, and nobody wrote songs about them (that I know of). Meanwhile, the Mods and life among them formed the basis of Peter Townshend's career.

Townshend, a self-admitted Mod, and his group The Who, legends in England long before their first American appearance, became champions of the Mod-experience. In years to come Townshend would go so far as to compose two major rock works about it, *Tommy, A Rock Opera,* in 1968 and *Quadrophenia,* his latest autobiographical creation and perhaps a leaving of it, in 1973.

"My Generation" is one of the first attempts by a songwriter in organized rock 'n' roll to identify the essence of his contemporaries from an insider's point of view. It is a bitter song. Where Jagger's rage was sexually (and perhaps economically) motivated, Townshend's was directed at society. Only Dylan was capable of such sentiments, but Dylan was not yet rock 'n' roll. Townshend had always been straight, hard rock, so his message cut deep.

The Mods were nihilistic, cynical before their time, out purely for pleasure in the form of parties and a pleasing mirror image . . . and in America too we were discovering that the pleasure principle was perhaps the one thing left in life not to be sneered at. When dope finally hit the colonies it hit hard because it felt so good; after the first few introductory tokes it became one of the primary tools for survival in an era of Vietnam, Civil Rights, and creeping repression.

So, even while the early Beatles were lullabying many into a love-happy daze, in other parts of the rock world the seeds of change and despair were in the wind.

"Help!" by Lennon and McCartney, 1965

It took awhile, but finally even the Beatles lost their virginity, and like the rest of the generation, somewhere along the way they ran into Bob Dylan, who opened their eyes to the world around them. Their immediate reaction was to cry for help, and shortly to pine for the good old days of "Yesterday."

But the ability to understand and change with the times was perhaps the Beatles' greatest asset. Whether it was the public that changed or the Beatles that changed the public, they were certainly right there at every spinning of the wheel. "Norwegian Wood" was considered a pioneering Beatle drug song. "Lucy In The Sky With Diamonds" indicated to many their ascent into LSD. They journeyed east with the sixties to discover a guru (the Rolling Stones never did that). And although they publicly decried the revolution (by violence, that is) they were the titular heads of the generation's grand attempt at unity— of folk and rock under the name of acid—and just coincidentally delivered one of the anthems of the time, called "Love Is All You Need." Sound familiar?

Dylan as a single artist offered the generation direction with each new change of his identity. The Beatles, as a group identity, picked up the clues from Dylan and translated them into language everyone could understand, even radio programmers. Together, for a time, they were an unstoppable force. They could have accomplished just about anything in the heyday of all this delirium; their words and music gave power to the fantasies of a hungry audience.

In the remaining years of the decade love would battle apathy, peace go up against violence, freedom encounter slavery at every crossroads. The skirmishes would bring us close to a revolution in mores, would dominate front-page headlines and would affect the politics of the nation. Many songwriters would rise to occasions here and there to document these valiant efforts, to keep the faithful hoping, on the streets, on the campuses, and in the living rooms of America.

Some of these same songwriters would also be around to chart the demise of these hopes, the failure of the music to keep afloat as the generation sank into the seventies faced with Dylan's retirement to country music and the Beatles' schizophrenic polarization into four individual identities—the dream was over.

It was at this time that a mass movement toward "Yesterday" got underway, hailed by industry and fans alike as the much welcomed Oldies Revival. One full step backward for rock 'n' roll.

PETER TOWNSHEND

Peter Townshend has always represented rock 'n' roll at its best: emotional, intuitive, energetic. Although somewhat over-shadowed in reputation by his illustrious contemporaries Mick Jagger, John Lennon, Ray Davies, and Paul McCartney, Town-

shend's songs certainly must rank as first-rate classics of the era, and his longer works will go down as the most ambitious use of the form to date.

Townshend's success in America is largely due to his rock opera *Tommy*—the story of a deaf, dumb, and blind pinball wizard who rises to legendhood—and *Quadrophenia*—based in part on autobiographical vignettes of the four members of his group, The Who, and also an epitaph for the Mod era in England.

In spite of his impressive body of work, most people think of Peter Townshend solely as the man who pioneered the act of demolishing his guitar onstage, initiating a rash of auto-destructive bands upon the public, a brief craze from which the musical instrument industry alone profited.

The interview with Peter Townshend took place in Los Angeles where the group was preparing for an evening show. Although I was the tenth and last interview of the day for Pete, he was still accommodating and pleasant. The topic of conversation, songwriting, was something he'd never discussed per se in an interview and he was quite interested in pursuing the matter.

"At age twelve or thirteen I wanted to get a guitar. My friend who wasn't very musical got his father, who was very clever, to make him a guitar. Not a musical instrument, just a sort of prop so he could stand in front of the mirror and pose around. It had piano strings and no frets and that sort of thing. And I used to go around to see him and I was actually able to play it in some way. And this guy's father used to say to me, 'Listen, if you can get any kind of music out of that, you'd probably make a very good guitar player, why don't you get a proper guitar?' So that Christmas my grandmother gave me this cheap guitar and I struggled away on that for about a year. Then I got a banjo and struggled away on that. Finally I got a good guitar. It was a slow transition.

"Another reason I played guitar initially is that I really did feel at the time it was going to be the only way that I was ever gonna get laid—to have a guitar and be in a group. One day somebody would sort of spot me and fall in love with me because I was a genius of a guitar player. I figured there was absolutely no point in me going out with the guys and going through the whole thing, 'Down At The Youth Club,' because I was not confident enough firstly, and I was not good looking enough secondly, which affects the first. And I knew bloody well that I was immature compared to a lot of other people, sort of stunted emotionally. So I felt that a couple of years stuck in a bedroom learning the guitar wouldn't do me any harm at all. So actually, when the other kids were out dancing or listening to records, I was learning the guitar."

Townshend described the scene "Down At The Youth Club."

"The Youth Club dances were often run by churches or guilds. You'd go down to the club and sit around and maybe ask somebody to jive, and all the girls seemed to be like five years older than the boys. You wore a suit and that kind of scene. In fact, it was at one of those clubs that I used to go to—it was run by the Congregational Church, so it got the subtitle, the Congo Club—that I first appeared on a stage, with John Entwistle playing trumpet and me playing banjo in a jazz group I think called the Scorpions, sort of unlikely name for a trad jazz group. We used to play Dixieland, stuff like 'Marching Through Georgia,' 'Farewell Blues,' and all that kind of stuff. And we stood up there—with about five people in the room—and I really blushed. It was the only time ever in my whole life that I've been nervous on a stage."

But was his sex life improving?

"What really changed things for me was going to art college. I could never believe that. I couldn't believe that all those *rules:* that you had to be good looking and smartly dressed, that you had to be intelligent and you mustn't ever pick your nose, that you had to always have something to say and you had to be big and you had to be strong; none of those unwritten rules applied in art college. Incredibly beautiful women would talk to you without needing to see your credentials. It took me about a year to get over that.

"I remember the first really crushing romance I had. It still brings tears to my eyes thinking about the lost romance that could have been in art college with an amazing woman, all because I just wasn't really prepared for it. Art college was where I sort of grew up. I had been going to a silly boys school, with silly girls running around, and all the silly, childish games that people play . . . and I walked into a thing where all that counted was what *really mattered*. It was pretty staggering.

"In *Quadrophenia* I wrote a song that didn't get included about this romance, this girl at school, and how I blew the relationship because I lied a lot. She was going out with a jazz musician and I was just like on the sidelines and I used to talk to her. I never thought there'd ever be a relationship but I used to like being in her presence and we used to sit next to one another, work and talk and eat together and that sort of thing. That was as far as it got. At the end of the day the jazz musician would come and pick her up and take her home.

"So I started to expand a bit on my musical capabilities in order to just perhaps bring myself into line a little bit with this other guy. Like, 'Well, I'm in a band and I play really well. I've got a number of guitars. I've worked with all kinds of people, all sorts of bands. I've got four or five different color jackets.' And we used to talk about jazz and stuff and I had a working knowledge about jazz because my father was a legitimate player; so I knew a little bit, but I didn't really know quite what I was talking about.

"The final boob was when her old man left her and she was very shattered by it, because he was older and she was very young, and she turned to me for emotional support, and apart from not being able to recognize it or being able to handle it . . . I got into a conversation about Charlie Parker, and said that I'd met him in a club and that he'd shaken my hand. It was a tragic thing. I remember it to this day. Because it was then she knew it was just not going to work. And what was tragic about it, looking back on it, was that she knew I was in the way of myself, that I really couldn't handle it.

"So I wrote a pretty song which we actually got to the point of laying down, called 'We Close Tonight.' The last verse of it is, 'I got three red jackets and a Fender Jazz and I play guitar in a mainstream band,' and the last line of the thing is, 'You could come and see us, but we close tonight.' But the humorous songs that I was writing seemed out of place somehow in *Quadrophenia*. They seemed too much like little funny cameos stuck in to lighten what was essentially a sad story. So I thought, well, fuck it, if it's gonna be sad, I might as well make it sad."

From there we moved into a discussion of *Quadrophenia*, Townshend's current work and its predecessor in the rock opera format, *Tommy*.

"I tend to think in trains of thought for maybe up to two years, which means that anything I write from now to say two years from now will probably end up with a similar purpose. I'll start to write a song and I won't really know what it's got to do with, then two years from now I'll look back on it and then I'll know why I wrote it. It might have some kind of catch thing that fits in with all the other stuff.

"I know when I put *Tommy* together I drew on all kinds of sources, and even in *Quadrophenia* there's quite a lot of material that came from earlier on that just fit. Every time I wrote I was writing about that kind of thing; adolescence or spiritual desperation. Also, last year, prior to the recording, I did really go through sort of a strange frame of mind. I did start to get a little bit desperate again, in an adolescent sense, that feeble clutching at some sort of sense of identity. For instance 'I'm One' was written in a genuine melancholic state.

"Then, in order to draw all the loose ends together, I have to sit down and do it. You know, I've got a studio in my house where I work and write, really, where I finish things off and organize music. It's like a 'den' in American terms. And I have to shut myself up in this room and work. I start to build up to it in a way so that it becomes sort of inevitable.

"What I do is force myself to do it by announcing things up front. *Tommy*, for example, I talked about at incredible length to Jann Wenner in a long, long article in Rolling Stone before I'd even finished writing it. I said so much that it just *had* to be finished—I had to get it done! I did the same thing with *Quadrophenia*. I announced it to everybody a long way ahead, so people started to build up to it.

"It's really good to do it that way, give somebody an idea. You can gauge your own enthusiasm. I mean it could be real genuine enthusiasm and involvement, or it could be an infatuation with an idea. So you can work it out by seeing how well you sell it to somebody else. And if you sell it really well you know that you're behind it. If you sell it to fifty people and you're still really up about it, then you know you're onto one that's going to get done.

"I had a lot of people say I shouldn't touch the opera form, and my argument then was that I wasn't. I wasn't really touching opera at all. Rock opera was a Kit Lambert phrase, a managerial term.

"But it's such a peculiar working process. Like often I pretend to everybody that I know what I'm doing when a lot of the time I really don't. I seem to think I do but I don't really . . . until things come together. That's why both *Tommy* and *Quadrophenia* haven't got properly conceived endings . . . because they were never properly conceived in front. They were allowed to happen in as spontaneous and easy a way, I hope, as a Buster Keaton two-reeler. Rather than something that was scripted in front and made to happen, it was allowed to happen. And if you didn't have an ending you didn't really care about it. You just had everybody walk off into the sunset.

"*Tommy* really came out too soon. There's so much I would change now, but we had to stop working on it. We'd been working on it a long time and we were sick of it. The last part of it was very rushed.

"The idea for *Quadrophenia* came to me about two years ago, in 1971, in November. Most of the really heavy things that ever happened to me have happened in November. I fell in love in November. I got stoned first in November. I had my first trip in November."

I asked Townshend to comment on the symbolism in his latest work.

"Symbolically, the rain in *Quadrophenia* is a blessing, like the thunder and the sea. They're all heavily symbolic in a structural sense and in an impressionistic sense, because the songs are songs. All that garbage in the mix, you know, that kind of thing we did just to impressionistically set things up so that the music seemed harder and shoved itself out more rather than just a series of songs that had to be listened to as cameos. And the rock in the ocean, the fact that it's in the ocean, like the island, is all fairly symbolic. I was very conscious of that kind of idea. The rock being most likely The Who, you know, something you could swim out from but you had to come back to it. And the ocean is like . . . everything. I mean universal in a mystical sense.

"I hope I've gotten that type of thing out of my system, because up to now I've written the same sort of thing, even in *Tommy* where I tried to take a stance *away*, where I tried to write about something that was a fantasy in a sense, it seemed to have a lot of familiar threads running through it, like family problems, the street social problems, like the bullying cousin Kevin, and the druggy things. I don't think up to now I've really been able to break loose from that sort of thing.

"But I'm really starting to get bored with adolescence and writing about it. I'm getting bored with kids and it's starting to become a sort of semi-senile middle-aged attitude toward adolescence. I don't feel at all ill at ease where I am. I don't feel I'm suffering from maturity. Actually, I'm quoting myself there, 'Suffering from maturity.' I was doing this interview in the Melody Maker where I said that. The best thing I ever said, that somebody *suffers* from maturity. I don't suffer from maturity, which I think is something that people consciously do. A lot of people walk around *acting* like adults. It's got nothing to do with morality or dignity. It's got nothing to do with that at all. I mean you can be free, or you can act stupidly, but you can still be dignified. And you can still be within the law sometimes. So I don't feel the need to celebrate adolescence anymore, that's all. I tried to make *Quadrophenia* feel like the last Who album of that type."

Townshend and The Who were always much more relevant in England to the street concerns of their peers than either the Stones or the Beatles. Most of his songs were based on the exploits and misadventures of his crowd—the Mods—and the pressures that affected their daily lives in the early sixties.

"I remember very clearly when 'My Generation' came out with the words 'I hope I die before I get old.' I kept on being asked, 'Do you really mean that, and if you're working in five years what do you think?' And I said, 'No way am I still going to be doing *anything* in five years!' I really believed that I was going to be dead.

"If you remember there was a huge atomic crisis through the Cuba thing . . . and I remember in England going to school one day *knowing* that the world was going to be blown to bits. And in college a lot of people were walking around like normal and occasionally one person would say, what the fuck are we doing all this for? Everybody was so resigned to it, they knew there was going to be an atomic war. No one looked like they were going to back down and that was just it. That was the kind of consciousness at the time. A lot of people have forgotten about it, but I remember the fucking feeling and it lasted for quite a number of years, when everybody was living 'in the shadow of the bomb' as it were, but they were totally resigned to it. If somebody had wanted to get me into narcotics strongly enough at that time, I think I would have gotten into it. Luckily nobody tried."

As the sixties progressed, Townshend became more socially involved in the politics of the time.

"I was in the 'Ban the Bomb' movement in England for a little while, the Young Communist League and stuff like that, but the thing that sort of bowled me over, like it did a lot of people, was LSD. It wiped me out a fantastic amount. I kind of stopped working and got very obsessed with it and really did believe that it was something enormous and incredibly important and was involved also with some of the sentiments surrounding it, the sort of love and peace thing.

"During that period I can only remember three songs that I wrote. Just pre my first acid trip I wrote 'Relax,' which ended up on one of our albums; 'Pictures Of Lily,' which was released as a single; and the other one I don't think anything happened to. And then, afterwards, I wrote some very weird songs. I wrote a song called 'Faith In Something Bigger,' that nothing ever happened to; 'Happy Jack'; and what became the 'Underture To *Tommy*' and 'Welcome' from *Tommy*. This is before I ever had the idea for *Tommy*."

I asked him which of the other English groups he respected or was influenced by.

"I was influenced a lot by the Stones. I've always felt Mick Jagger to be much older—he's thirty, two years older than me, but he's always felt a lot older . . . maybe that's because they were a bigger group. But I liked almost everything they did. I also liked a lot of the Beatles stuff but I was never influenced that much by it. I mean musically they just seemed to have such a peculiar method of working, and also a lot of it was melodic in a way although it sounded great when they did it. When you tried to find out what it was that made it tick and react to it musically, it was very sort of Italian lovesongs sort of stuff. Like 'Yesterday' and that stuff. How can you be influenced by that?

"Ray Davies is one of my favorite writers. His stuff is a bit heavily nostalgic but I still really like it. I was quite keen on Elton John—I really liked some of the writing approach on his *Elton John* album. I didn't entirely realize at the time that it was a two-man show. That weakened it for me, that took the sting out of it."

I asked then about American writers, but the best Townshend could do was to come up with someone Canadian born—Joni Mitchell.

"Joni Mitchell I really liked; then again I don't always listen to the words. What gets me is the sound rather than the actual lyrics. But she writes so personally. You know, she writes about things that are so secret. I sort of shy away from that a little bit. I'm deeply in love with her though.

"I find writing fairly much an unconscious thing. It doesn't involve that much effort, so I don't need much stimulation. I don't really look around for it. And if I like something usually I like it pretty much at face value."

Next we discussed his humble beginnings as a songwriter.

"Almost from the first time I put pen to paper I was a successful writer. 'Can't Explain' got into the British charts. It was kind of a lift off the feeling the Kinks had in 'You Really Got Me.' But the words . . . I suppose in a way it's a moon and June song. 'I think it's love, gonna say to you when I feel blue. . . .' I thought later, yeah, it's got nothing to do with love at all, it's got to do with a whole lot of other things. But that was only in retrospect.

"I discovered then that I had this ability to just sit down and scribble things out and think that I was writing consciously. But the real meaning was coming from somewhere else that I had absolutely no control over. Like odd things would give me an incredible surprise. I suppose I was surprised by how obviously observant I was, without ever really being conscious of it.

" 'Anyway, Anyhow, Anywhere' was the second song that I

wrote. It was modified a bit by Roger Daltry; that's why he shares a credit with me. Those two songs I wrote while I was living in complete squalor, getting stoned every night and listening to Jimmy Reed records. Anyway, anyhow, anywhere. Those were just three words I wrote on a piece of paper; you know, you used to do that when you were stoned out of your head. You look at it the next day and say, what the fuck was I talking about? Those three words were what I wrote to describe the way Charlie Parker plays—anyway, anyhow, anywhere. So that became the title for our next single, which was required the statutory two weeks after the release of the first one. I knocked out the song and it was much more of a conscious thing. I already looked back at 'I Can't Explain' and I started to think, yeah, this one's gonna be about a punk kid.

"About a year after that Kit Lambert started announcing to everyone that he thought I was a genius. I mean I produced a fantastic amount of demos. I holed up in my flat with two tape machines, writing consistently. Kit often used to fantasize about doing something on a grand scale even then. I mean it was his idea to do the mini opera on the *Quick One, Happy Jack* album in the States. It was him pushing me to do grander things in a way. So even if I wasn't getting written about as a great writer, Kit Lambert was telling me I was a great writer and I believed him, because I wanted to believe him.

"There were other people that I respected that liked our music. Jagger really liked it and said so, which was encouraging. The Beatles really liked the *Quick One* album. Paul McCartney was saying that they were in the recording studio—at that time they would have been recording *Sergeant Pepper*—and they heard that album and really liked it and were doing something similar, and that was affecting what they were doing, which I thought was very nice.

"Funnily enough, I did write a couple of songs very early in the band's career. Keith Moon wasn't even with us then. We were doing Beatle songs and stuff like this and I wrote two songs; one was called 'It was You' and the other one I Can't even remember. But the group used to do them and they used to be quite well received in the little pubs we used to play in. Then I laid off writing for a long, long time, about two years altogether, and we started to get into rhythm and blues. Then the Stones came on the scene and they sort of affirmed that we were all right with rhythm and blues, so we got even more into it. And when we went for a recording audition with EMI, they said they liked the band but they felt we needed original material.

"This was pre our contact with the real situation of the kids on the street. It was pre our playing places like the Goldhawk Club, Sheperd's Bush—a sort of local marquee club—and stuff like that. I mean we used to play pubs and social clubs, but the Mod movement wasn't really underway. It was happening then but it wasn't quite solid, and although I knew what it was to be stoned, I wasn't really into the pep pill ideology, the sped-up thing that went along with the Mods.

"Actually, EMI could very well have said, they'll make a good R 'n' B band, cause a little bit later a lot of R 'n' B bands did get recording contracts, people like Mayall and Georgie Fame, just on the strength of their covering other R 'n' B material.

"So it never really occurred to me to write; it was more EMI's idea. Actually I'm deeply indebted to them."

KEITH REID

With the astounding success of the Beatles, the nature of song-writing changed. No longer could songs be mass produced in Brill Building cubicles here and abroad, thrown into a vat for

hungry groups to dive in after. Now the groups were writing their own material and just the fact that it was written by them lent a certain raw credibility to even the lamest lyrics. The market for the glossy, three-minute, Oscar-nominee-type Tin Pan Alley number dwindled down to a precious Andy Williams few.

There was a flaw in the waxworks, however, in assuming that every good songwriter was also a performer. Many writers had no desire to add on another career. Some gave up the writing of lyrics in favor of prose. After all, an author is not expected to star in the movie made from his novel, is he? Until that point lyrics and performing had seemed to be at opposite ends of the music spectrum—one the sedentary, lonely craft; the other more the lampshade center of attention—although it is true that many lyricists were frustrated performers, which the remaining years of the sixties more than bore out.

Because, what happened was, convinced by their producers, agents, allies, and best friends, egged on by the success of Bob Dylan and Phil Ochs, a whole bunch of writers decided to go on record and on tour as performers, much like poets reading their own work. And only poets can get the proper nuances across, right? So we had Leonard Cohen, Randy Newman, Neil Young, Loudon Wainwright—all primarily known first as poets, second as singers, and then loosely defined as such. The era of the ordinary but emotionally charged voice was born among non-singing singers everywhere. It caught on.

But there was a second cluster of writers, who still couldn't bring themselves to face an audience, who did things the hard way. They moved in with a group and wrote songs with the lead guitarist. Or they found a singer and wrote his words for him. Primarily linear poets, these writers, one must assume, wrote the words first, possibly even had a backlog of poems which, with the addition of melody, became the songs of the mid-to-late sixties.

Numbered among this group are Robert Hunter, of the

Grateful Dead (who recently succumbed to releasing an album of his own), Bernie Taupin (who writes the script for Elton John), and Keith Reid, perhaps the first of these linear poets, in conjunction with Procol Harem, who helped usher in the pscheldic age. (A psychedelic song was any song whose lyrics were sufficiently imagistic or complex or vague as to defy immediate interpretation and therefore to suggest that it was written to or about or under the influence of a mind-expanding drug.)

The following comment was supplied to me by Keith Reid in response to a letter I sent him.

"My method of writing is something like the construction of a jigsaw puzzle without knowing what the finished picture will be.

"I start off with one or two pieces i.e. a phrase ('Grand Hotel') or fragments of a concept ('Man's selfdestruction' which was developed into 'As Strong As Samson'—or 'love which has burnt itself out and turned into fending and bitterness' as in 'Fires Which Burnt Brightly'). Then, by interlocking pieces into the original parts, I build up a picture that makes sense, and conveys my thoughts, and meaning.

"Originally I made a pattern—a theme of work, or a story, but behind it was always a joy in the use and sound of words for themselves. Over the years I have come to reject the use of words for themselves alone more and more, and as a result of this, theme and story line have become more important. My work has become simplified—more primitive if you like. I cut away as much of the fat as possible, and try to leave the bare bones."

PART FOUR

Back in the U.S.A.:
1963–1966

(Street Action)

Southern California

"Surfin' USA," by Brian Wilson, 1963

Contrary to popular opinion, American-made rock 'n' roll did not go into a terminal deep freeze because of the British invasion—it only seemed that way. A closer look reveals that musically America was opening up as never before, with different parts of the country offering tasty, homemade musical dishes in their own unique style—often dictated by the cities where the music originated, the street life of the natives who lived and listened there.

In Southern California at the time, rock 'n' roll equalled surfing. Everybody and his cat named dog was into the first major athletic craze since bowling. Until 1963 most people (especially Easterners) considered surfing a sport on a par with skydiving and wrestling alligators. But trust California to make it popular! Brian Wilson wrote "Surfin' USA," and pretty soon kids in Kansas were breaking up their local playgrounds so they could surf in the backyard swimming pool.

The Beach Boys, Jan and Dean, the Surfaris, the Marketts, the Hondells, Ronny and the Daytonas all came to symbolize the California look, which soon melted into the California image—tall, tanned, blond; with long hair, a fixed smile, perfect teeth, and a 73 I.Q. Mindless sunworshippers, athletes, beautiful boys and girls wearing bikinis; the clean teens as opposed to the scruffy East Coast beatnik folksinging protesters.

The Beach Boys could have been the Four Freshmen. Their songs spoke for all those who were pleasant chaps, always the gentleman with a lady (until they got her in the back seat of their Corvette). They sang about California adolescence: surfing, driving cars, being true to your school, the joys of having a room of your own. They were the ultimate suburbanites in the ultimate suburb—Los Angeles—speaking for that great washed majority in America who longed for the old-fashioned values, the simple choices—mom, apple pie, and virginity.

This majority began to look, if only in fantasy, toward California as their land of possibility, not to Hollywood as in the past, but to the beach, by the surf; an easygoing lifestyle in white slacks, white half-sneakers, no socks.

Detroit

"Dancing in the Streets," by Holland, Dozier, Holland, 1964
Through the courtesy of the Motown record label in Detroit, black America began to find the voice it had seemingly lost in 1956. Because of certain pioneering writers like Eddie Holland, Smokey Robinson, and Curtis Mayfield the people of the country became aware that there were *black* teen-agers too. Also, black teen-agers themselves became aware that they existed to whites. In Diana Ross and the Supremes, Smokey and the Miracles, Curtis and the Impressions, Martha and the Vandellas, Mary Wells, Little Stevie Wonder, a new breed of hero was offered to a segment of the generation which had been most often in the past merely swept under the rug of popular opinion.

Basically, the black lyricists proved to be as preoccupied with love as any white writers, but they were far more dire about it. Anyone following Diana Ross and the Supremes from heartbreak to heartbreak (as written by Eddie Holland and company) couldn't fail to be moved by her soap operatic shifts of fortune. "Where Did Our Love Go?" she complains, before yearning for a "Baby Love," a return to innocence. Her travails continued through "Stop! In The Name Of Love," but were mercifully put to an end with "Back In My Arms Again." Still, we knew that tomorrow would ultimately bring pain . . . and sure enough, a few weeks later she was back in traction singing "Nothing But Heartaches," an epic of frustrated desires.

Martha and the Vandellas didn't fare much better. Being in love to them was like being caught in "Quicksand." Later on they requested everyone join them "Dancing In The Streets," but that was only because they had "Nowhere To Run" (again written by E. Holland) in which they say it's not love they're running from, "but the heartbreak I know will come . . ."

In the midst of this passion and frustration, Smokey Robinson was coolly extolling the virtues of "My Girl" and having Mary Wells pay back the compliment with his "My Guy," a lyric expressing her faithfulness in a time of mass heartbreak for the rest of the Motown crew. The Four Tops (as scripted by Holland–Dozier–Holland once more) certainly couldn't identify with Smokey's outlook, even if, personally, they were all nice guys. They emerged song after song as bottom dog in a one-sided love affair, such as in the typical "I Can't Help Myself," followed a few months later (while Dylan and the Beatles were revolutionizing the charts) with "The Same Old Song," still suffering now that the latest affair had ended in disaster.

Eventually all this bottled up sexual frustration would have to reach a natural boiling point. In Detroit one summer the teakettle blew its top. The racial tension and the riots which took place there foretold the great black identity crisis which would dominate American lives (to say nothing of American Top Ten charts) in cities everywhere for the rest of the sixties and the early years of the seventies as well.

On the other side of the tracks from Motown, quite a different message was being prepared. Typified by a group called the MC5 and known as early Heavy Metal, this message was extreme, the radical fringe of rock 'n' roll—a destructive element. The MC5 were loud, their lyrics strident. "Kick Out The Jams" is the only song I remember of theirs, advising the audience to wreck the place as soon as the 5 got all their expensive equipment out of there.

This "wreck the place" mentality would gain prominence and importance as the sixties went by and the action in Vietnam went on unabated. Thousands of frustrated, impotent white kids would do just that when they realized they had little chance of making an impact on society any other way. The combined forces, black power and radical politics, would do as much to put the country on edge in post-1965 America as the bomb and threats of the bomb had prior to 1963.

Los Angeles

"I Got You Babe," by Sonny Bono, 1965
When the riots finally hit L.A., America knew the easy days had come to a close. In Watts the bubble burst with a vengeance . . . and on Sunset Strip weirdly dressed young people, reeking of dope, paraded for solidarity. The cardboard food and car culture, spawned by the city on the Freeway, had turned upon itself in great waves of looting. America's psychotic quest for products had led to this cohabitation in violent display by our productless and anti-product minorities, blacks and hippies.

On the radio it was folk/rock with a vengeance, California's answer to protest music. Barry McGuire, an ex-New Christy Minstrel, recorded the savage "Eve of Destruction," which warned the rabble against imminent destruction from every conceivable angle (and a few pretty inconceivable ones), sentiments which those in the East were already far beyond . . . but it was certainly a daring message to be contained in a *number one hit song!* West Coast legends-to-be, the Byrds, also hit number one in 1965 with Dylan's drug-lyric "Mr. Tamborine Man" and followed it with a message from the Bible and Pete Seeger, "Turn, Turn, Turn," a theological discourse on changes. Transplanted New Yorkers, the Turtles, growled another of Dylan's gems of disaffection "It Ain't Me Babe," a violent reaction to the demands a relationship made on personal freedom. Sonny and Cher did a Dylan imitation (in their ragamuffin pre Steve and Eydie phase), "I Got You Babe," complete with nasal drawl. And deep in the L.A. shadows, "madman" (ex-adman) Frank Zappa was writing of eerie new beings "Hungry Freaks," and "Who Are The Brain Police?" offering an acid vision of the future. A future coming closer everyday.

If Los Angeles was the dream center of middle-America fantasy life, then that fantasy life came apart at the seams. The children of edge city, smack up against the wall of the sea, the black man running wild in the shopping center—the solid foundation on which their lives had been built was proving to be rotten from the bottom up. And there was no way to keep this news off the nation's airwaves.

Eddie Arnold attempted to provide an adult perspective in all the clamor with his rendition of "Make The World Go Away," but although that attitude might certainly have worked in the past, this was a new generation. For the remainder of the sixties the world would be very much with us and never more strongly focused on the young, for better or worse.

And while Annette Funicello and Frankie Avalon (those good teens you never hear about) tried to redirect attention to the funloving kids on the beach playing bingo, America *really* knew that all was lost to the other side when the spotless Beach Boys gave indications of defecting to the alternate culture. "Good Vibrations" not only picked up on code language and sounded as if the Boys had gotten their heads together . . . but it might possibly have been their finest minutes.

San Francisco

"Get Together," by Dino Valenti, 1965
When the wave of the future broke, it hit further up the coast in San Francisco, previously known as Pacific headquarters for the beat generation and ranked just ahead of Denver as one-two mystic cities of the West. By 1965 all the beatniks had left North Beach and the neighborhood was past its prime as a meeting ground for anyone but Midwestern businessmen–tourists (with their wives and/or clients). Ferlinghetti's City Lights Bookstore had become a relic of a forgotten time among progressive topless shoeshine parlors, bottomless nightclubs and transvestite cabarets.

The new age arrived in the mountains to the north via Ken
Kesey, pioneering acid activist, and his jolly bunch of friends
and media freaks known as the Merry Pranksters. Their periodic
music and LSD festivals, thrown at Kesey's mountain hideaway,
later became the standard dance-form happening of the sixties
as experienced (with flashing strobes, psychedelic lights and
acid/rock) at San Francisco's Avalon Ballroom and New York's
Balloon Farm, later Electric Circus . . . and thenceforth at
isolated side-of-the-road dives up and down the American
psychedelic highway by 1967.

The rumblings of something weird filtered down and were
picked up in the city; a little four-square funky section of
town called Haight–Ashbury took up the cause, waved its freak
flag high, and extended the emerging trip from dope to acid,
from folk/rock to hallucination. Every night packs of freaks
came to unite on the corner of Haight and Ashbury, to drop,
rap, fall out, flake out, or talk music.

It was here the democratic concept of music of the people,
by the people, for the people . . . and for free, truly started.
The Grateful Dead played just up the street at the Straight
Theatre. The Jefferson Airplane's famous house was across the
park. Everyone knew at least one freak who claimed to have
lived next door to Janis Joplin. Every Sunday these groups and
others played in the park for free; the people tripped on
acid; the vibes were mellow.

By day the Haight was home for freaks of all denomination.
Long of hair, bare of feet, stopping off to purchase their
necessities at incense and candle factories; leather and jewelry
stands; belt, boot, and beaderies. Multicolored people painted
with day-glo. Fifteen-year-old girls panhandling. (Incidentally,
panhandling, in the latter part of the sixties would come to
replace the paper route as the number one source of subteen
income.) Everybody lived twelve to a brownstone in peace and
acid bliss. (This period also saw the rise of the bulletin board–
index card as the new community newspaper—notice of rides

needed, free kittens, a bass-player [preferably gay] wanted . . . and mostly calls for roommates: three females desire male for two room apartment.) It was a freewheeling, loose, and rolling time, and if you listened you could hear rock music coming from every basement window.

As the Indians survived by mass producing blankets, the hippies made do by selling their handmade goods in Head Shoppes and were supported, while it lasted, by the curious tourists.

In all this Dino Valenti was a certified underground legend. A hush would fall over every coffeehouse in which his name was spoken and last for nearly half a minute. Singers who did "Get Together" generally earned twice as much as the others when the hat was passed around.

In 1965, according to whom you talked to, Valenti was either dead, in jail, or hiding out at sea. By the time he did reappear, with a band of his own named Quicksilver Messenger Service, "Get Together" had become the national anthem of the Hippie Kingdom. In 1968, long after the hippie had been officially pronounced dead, "Get Together," as done by the Youngbloods, became the national habit.

Greenwich Village

"Like A Rolling Stone," by Bob Dylan, 1965
"Do You Believe In Magic?" by John Sebastian, 1965
Perhaps the most crucial chapter in the history of rock 'n' roll can be summed up in the phrase: Dylan Goes Electric.

Furor! Scandal! Sell-out! Fink!

A community of purists arose, acoustic guitars up in arms, storming the holy barricades of Newport. A generation that had chosen this new form of folk music to express its innermost passions, which had drawn a sacred line between itself and the barbarians of rock 'n' roll (even the delightful, toe-tapping refrains of the Beatles were dismissed by them as essentially trivial) recoiled in pain to see one of their own, their leader, their voice, now trading riffs with the *other side*. Dylan up there on the stage with an electric rock 'n' roll band. Dylan, backed by such as organist Al Kooper. The same Al Kooper who had been in the Royal Teens, sung on "Short Shorts," actually collaborated in the writing of "This Diamond Ring," for crying out loud! It was nothing short of heresy. Rock 'n' roll had been officially declared passé by the elite; no Beatles, no Stones, no Ruby and the Romantics could ever restore its prior glory. But in one deft move Dylan broke through all that, and while he was at it, ushered in rock's Golden Age.

Word had it he'd been hanging around with the Beatles, over in England.

Not that it was so easy, even for Dylan. At Forest Hills in New York, soon after his Newport rock debut, he opened up with an acoustic set amid rumbles of his coming defection brought down from returning folkies. When his second set began, in full regalia, with a backbeat, the rumbles turned to a roar of scorn. Dylan had to walk off the stage in mid-set, in mid-song (possibly in mid-sentence). But he did manage to introduce the eerie gem "Ballad Of A Thin Man," in which he told his audience that something was happening right before their eyes and they didn't know what it was! Dylan always communicated with his audience that way; cryptically, through his songs. Not two months later, at Carnegie Hall, all the new converts were cheering his every word. And outside, ex-folkies were adding electric pickups to their guitars and an entourage of rock 'n' roll accompanists to follow them from studio to coffeehouse to folk festival.

Those who never left MacDougal Street were witness to a joyful transformation. Regular followers of the hoot night scene at the Gaslight, the Bitter End, and Folk City and fledgling Bohemians, who spent their Sundays around the fountain in Washington Square listening to Brooklyn banjo pickers trying to sound Appalachian, had grown up with the music.

To hear folk/rock on the radio, to see it reach the top of the national charts, was a vindication sweet to savor. Our side was winning.

As in the Haight, nights in the Village were carnivals: hippies and straights, cops and pickpockets, tourists and Long Island freaks, along with the original Italian residents; a ceaseless parade of winos, junkies, motorcycle goons, and gypsy girls who seemed to offer secret sensual revelations (but never did), the frequent glimpse of Dylan *just walking down the block,* Figaro's and the Night Owl. The Night Owl café meant three things: one, Richie Havens; two, Buzzy Linhart (sometimes Tim Hardin or *Fred Neil*); and three, John Sebastian and the Lovin' Spoonful.

John Sebastian will always be thought of as a kind of big brother figure of the period, known for his flamboyant polo shirts (as well as his incredible harmonica belt). Before Sebastian got done with the generation he would manage to push back the boundaries of adolescence to the age of thirty, making it acceptable to rush home and air out those old dungarees and polo shirts not worn since high school. His collection of rock 'n' roll classics, all penned for the Spoonful, can be likened to that same reclaiming of childhood joy.

Although the wide tie certainly gave it a spirited run for its money, the dominance of the polo shirt (along with trusty Lees, Levis, and Wranglers) as the favorite item of clothing of the counterculture (after a brief skirmish with the turtleneck, which eventually made the leap into polite society) has remained unchallenged. Together with dungarees they have helped the generation ward off the white shirt and tie of the middle-aged.

Chicago

"Born in Chicago," by Nick Gravenites, 1965
Long before rock 'n' roll, there was blues. Down South they'd been singing it forever, sometimes even on record—Robert

Johnson, Lightning Hopkins, Skip James, Mississippi John Hurt, Son House. Obscure practitioners of the art whose works acquired a dedicated following among whites at Newport and nearly nowhere else.

Suddenly, however, in the mid-to-late sixties, great masses of middle-class white kids turned to the blues. On the southside of Chicago veterans like Muddy Waters, Howling Wolf, Junior Wells and Buddy Guy, Homesick James and the Dusters all experienced an incredible surge of popularity. Maybe the Civil Rights movement had led to an increased study and identification of black culture; maybe the roots of rock were finally showing through . . . whatever the reasons, blues arrived.

And the charge was led by Paul Butterfield and his Chicago Blues Band. Following them, a battalion of blues-based hard/rock bands would overrun the sixties. Descendants of these second-generation groups can be heard in the seventies going under the name of Heavy Metal and called Brownsville Station, Black Oak Arkansas, and Blue Oyster Cult.

Blues/rock was much tougher than regular rock, a lyric born of a deeper experience. The blues image concerned living in tenements, in basements, in slums with rats; while rock 'n' roll was still living at home with parents (and later on in communes on acid). If rock 'n' roll was dungarees and polo shirts, blues was a black shirt and a white tie, a return to grease.

Better known for its piercing guitarists than its piercing lyricists, blues/rock gave birth to the sixties great guitar debates (replacing in hip circles the one time great centerfielder baseball debate). Who was better? Mike Bloomfield or Danny Kalb or Eric Clapton or Johnny Winter or Jimi Hendrix? Everyone had a favorite; learning guitarists memorized licks the way English majors recall lines of nineteenth-century verse.

Blues/rock became the music of the sixties hipster, proving for its generation to be more direct than jazz; a catharsis for the repressed children of the fifties. Mick Jagger teased them with "Let's Spend The Night Together," but John Hammond gave them an orgasm with "Squeeze my lemons till the juice runs down my leg . . ." undoubtedly from an old Robert Johnson blues.

These were not sentiments for the squeamish; the adolescent turned away, created imitation blues-seeming groups like Deep Purple and Blue Cheer, which possessed noise and little else to move the senses. But by the decade's end, these same younger brothers and sisters would be creating their own nightmare statements via something called deca/rock also known as punk/rock . . . derived from their early scathing encounters with The Blues.

Nashville

"Harper Valley PTA," by Tom T. Hall, 1968
Although by 1966 it may have seemed that the whole world was watching the counterculture, that was at least a year away. In actuality *most* of the world was still listening to good old country and western music . . . the heartbeat of the common foot soldier in life's National Guard, the sound of Middle America. It was booze music for late night lonesome losers. Truckstop tunes on the jukebox, a dime a dance, impress the waitress.

Nearly all C&W tunes were written about booze (the great American drug), loose women, or unfaithful husbands . . . or a combination of the three. Sometimes they were about hopping freights and sometimes they were about religion, but usually about the poor sap who got so drunk that he messed around with a loose woman and his wife kicked him out of the house . . . so he took to religion after a gin-soaked meeting with a Baptist minister in the baggage compartment of a northbound freight.

In Nashville—Tin Pan Alley South—talented C&W writers still turned out patented three-minute gems of the genre, but by the late sixties, something weird happened to country music. First Bobbie Gentry did the mysterious "Ode To Billie Joe," a song which probably defies interpretation (and leaves unanswered the question: What was in the package the two doomed lovers threw from the Tallahatchie Bridge? We may never know). Then Jeannie C. Riley proved in Harper Valley that Peyton Place existed elsewhere than the East. Bobby Goldsboro's "Honey," in 1968 also, advanced C&W to new heights of the maudlin with a soapy tale of a young wife who died (and this *prior* to *Love Story*). In 1970, John Hartford made poetry of the simple act of running away in "Gentle On My Mind," while in 1971 Kris Kristofferson's celebration of the open road "Me And Bobbie McGee," became a contemporary classic, sung to Bobbies of both sexes. In the rise of such C&W poets as Tom T. Hall and John Prine, who deal in story songs about the forgotten men and women of Middle America, we see a sensibility approximating that of a songwriting William Faulkner. To bring us right up to date, 1973 has seen Vicki Lawrence score with "The Night The Lights Went Out In Georgia," which in one song managed to bring together everything short of gothic horror (murder, political corruption, newlyweds, mistaken identity, backwoods justice, and a touch of incest) to make its point. And Helen Reddy had perhaps the hit of the year with Alex Harvey's "Delta Dawn," about a disturbed, if not retarded, local girl who had certainly stepped off the deep end once too often.

All of this going to show that the people of the country and West had finally awakened to the fact that even common folks, if unleashed, had a sick strain in them that would rival that of the fiercest hippie.

Philadelphia

"South Street," by Mann and Appel, 1963
Philly had been deserted ever since our favorite square, Dick Clark, left town for Disneyland with Frankie and Fabian, drop-

ping Paul Anka and Bobby Rydell off in Las Vegas. In the late sixties the town would again emerge as a center when Kenny Gamble and Leon Huff would create Philly-soul, a soft, laid-back R&B, the prevailing beat for street life in the seventies. But in the mid-sixties if anyone thought of Philadelphia it was to consider attending the Philly Folk Festival.

This festival came to rival Newport once Newport got out of hand, with hippies roaming the streets and rock bands invading the lair of the purist. When Newport finally fell, Philly remained as the final outpost of traditional folk music.

The scene there was pastoral, never too crowded, a weekend retreat where Bill Monroe and the Bluegrass Boys could play side by side with Koerner, Ray, and Glover and nose to nose with John Denver and the Mitchell Trio. Where John Sebastian appeared with his legendary harmonica belt.

When the confrontations in the cities came, when free-form radio brought experimental rock to the masses, when middle-class young America, black and white, freaked out . . . only Philadelphia remained pure and untouched. But of course, that was only for a short time.

Harvard Square–Berkeley

"Urge For Going," by Joni Mitchell, 1966
In college towns across the country, the undergrads were getting restless. In the fifties they'd been content to overrun Fort Lauderdale come Easter and be done with it, and in the early sixties destroying Newport was a good way to let off steam; but around 1966, students were blowing up every day. The entire college establishment (like the war establishment, the sex establishment, the authority establishment) became fair game for takeover. Students protested any and every aspect of the college experience, from prices in the lunch room to the core of the curriculum to the right to say four letter words (like *help*) in

public. In some cases college officials bent or broke, in others they called for the National Guard.

The most radical of the students risked their academic careers over issues they felt relevant. The less committed merely dropped out to face the perils of real life (including the perils of the draftboard). By the thousands they took to apartments in Cambridge, in Berkeley, in New York City, in San Francisco. And by the thousands they dreamed of the freedoms to be tasted on the open road.

Joni Mitchell was at that time a coffeehouse singer of local legend in the Detroit area and of high esteem in and around Greenwich Village. Her "Urge For Going," as sung in those parts by Tom Rush, was a chilling evocation of the paralysis which gripped the snowbound dreamer in the mid-sixties faced with so many life-changing choices which the autumn always seemed to put before you. Another year of school . . . or freedom at last? There had to be someplace to escape the chill of winter, to find life affirmed rather than denied. It was not so surprising, then, where this sunshine turned out to be.

New York City

"California Dreamin'," by John Phillips, 1966
Once again California proved the answer, America's golden mean. Go West young man and woman, for expansion of the mind, freedom for the body and soul. The early troubles had been forgotten and the sun was still shining. Joni Mitchell found her way out there to watch the remainder of the sixties from the other end zone. John Sebastian packed his wife and family and took off with his harmonicas and his trunk of polo shirts. In California, so they said, one could wear polos well into old age. Phil Ochs sent us a letter; come on down the weather's fine.

Little by little, inch by inch, the generation moved closer to that promised garden, causing the remaining Eastern stalwarts to be hard pressed to hang on in the cold.

As the sixties stumbled toward their denouement, California would be the scene of the best and worst effects of the generation: some fine songwriting in the works of Joni Mitchell, Randy Newman, and Jackson Browne; some notable bad trips inspired by politics, acid, and Charles Manson.

FRANK ZAPPA

Although primarily considered a composer, Frank Zappa's lyrics reflect his unique approach to rock 'n' roll almost as well as his music does. Combining a Theater of the Absurd sensibility, sharp-edged satiric humor, and a hair-trigger threshold of outrage, his odes to teen-age life, set in a fifties backbeat, are classics of the snide put-down.

Always in the vanguard of modern music, Zappa was the first (and is still perhaps the only) musician to bring a classical orientation to the form, producing pieces which certainly might be thought of as symphonic rhythm and blues.

With his group, The Mothers of Invention, in the summer of 1967 (the infamous Summer of Love), Frank Zappa brought a wicked and spontaneous theatricality to the rock stage at the Garrick Theatre, long before anyone else was doing it.

Since then Zappa has extended his vision further into the realms of classical music, rock, jazz, and R&B. He has also become involved with films (*200 Motels*).

Known for his hostility to reporters, Zappa was nonetheless quite cordial in our meeting at the Golden Gate Motel in Brooklyn, overlooking scenic Sheepshead Bay.

"I didn't start listening to music until I was about fifteen years old because my parents weren't too fond of it, and we didn't have a radio or a record player or anything. I think the

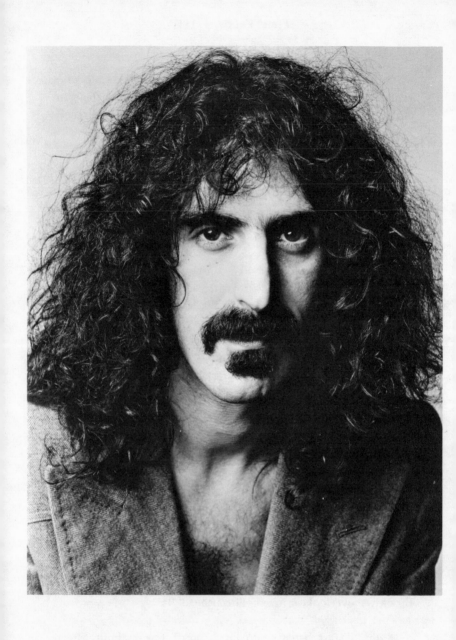

first music that I heard that I liked was Arab music and I don't know where I ever ran into it, but I heard it someplace and that got me off right away. Then I heard a song called 'I' by the Velvets on the Red Robin label and 'Gee' and 'Sh-boom,' 'Riot In Cell Block Number Nine,' and 'Annie Had A Baby.' By accident I heard those things and they knocked me out.

"I didn't start writing songs per se until I was about twenty years old, twenty-one maybe, because all my compositions prior to that time had been orchestral or chamber music. I think the basic idea of being a composer is if you're going to be true to yourself and write what you like, you write what you like without worrying whether it's going to be academically suitable or whether it's going to make any mark in history or not. My basic drive for writing anything down is I want to hear it.

"The very first tunes that I wrote were fifties Doo-wop. 'Memories Of El Monte' and stuff like that. It's always been my contention that the music that was happening during the fifties has been one of the finest things that ever happened to American music and I loved it. I could sit down and write a hundred more of the nineteen-fifties-type songs right now and enjoy every minute of it. I think my writing is as influenced, however, by country blues as it is by nineteen-fifties stuff. I've always been fond of Muddy Waters, Lightning Slim, Howling Wolf, and those guys.

"At the time I was living in a part of town called Echo Park [Los Angeles] which was a Mexican, Japanese, Filipino, Black neighborhood and I lived in a little two-room place, grubby little place on the side of a hill, 1819 Bellevue Avenue. In that house I wrote 'Brain Police,' 'Oh No, I Don't Believe It,' 'Hungry Freaks,' 'Bowtie Daddy,' and five or six others. A lot of the songs off the first album [*Freak Out*] had already been written for two or three years before the album came out. And a lot of songs wouldn't come out until the third or fourth album.

"About fifty percent of the songs were concerned with the

events of 1965. Los Angeles, at that time, in the kiddie community that I was hanging out in, they were all getting into
acid very heavily and you had people seeing God in colors and
flaking out all over the place. You had plenty of that and meanwhile there was all that racial tension building up in Watts.

"I was up to San Francisco once or twice, but I wasn't interested or influenced by the scene there. Basically I thought
what was happening in San Francisco in that early stage was . . .
well, I'll tell you what I saw when I went there. Whereas in
L.A. you had people freaking out; that is, making their own
clothes, dressing however they wanted to dress, wearing their
hair out; that is, being as weird as they wanted to be in public
and everybody going in separate directions—I got to San
Francisco and found everybody dressed up in 1890s garb, all
pretty specific codified dress. It was like an extension of high
school, where one type of shoe is the 'in' shoe, belt-in-the-back
peggers, or something like that. It was in the same sort of vein,
but it was the costume of the 1890s. It was cute, but it wasn't
as evolved as what was going on in L.A. In San Francisco they
had a 'more rustic than thou' approach."

From there Zappa and The Mothers moved on to New York
in the summer of 1967.

"There wasn't too much going on in the Village that interested me. The people who came to see us at the Garrick mostly
had short hair; they came from middle-class white Jewish en-
vironments, mostly suburban. They came to see our show because we were something weird that was on that street and
we were a sort of specialized recreational facility.

"The reason they were shocked in those days was that they
hadn't seen or heard anything that came close to what we were
doing. Now, after so many groups imitating various aspects of
what we did, they've seen it from other sources. Take, for instance, Alice Cooper. Basically what they're doing is a cos-
meticized version of the same thing we were doing in 1967. He's

taken the obvious showmanship aspects without doing the difficult musical things. By simplifying the music to the point where you don't have to worry about it too much, and doing it with a lot of lights and a lot of props, you can put together a show that can have wider appeal."

Eventually our discussion shifted to his feelings about lyric writing.

"I think that by the time I put a lyric down on a piece of paper and go through all the drudgery of setting it to a musical format and rehearsing it and so forth . . . that they're all reasonably successful in saying what they were intended to say. There's plenty more that could be said, but there are mechanical obstacles in the way of getting that out to an audience. I think there are lots of things that I'd love to be able to express to people in lyrics, but being sort of a rational person I sit down and figure out, do those people really want to know, and is it worth the trouble to write it out, rehearse it, perform it night after night, record it . . . just to express my point of view on a subject when it's none of my business to inform somebody else about it in the first place.

"Basically what people want to hear in a song is I love you, you love me; I'm o.k. you're o.k.; the leaves turn brown, they fell off the trees; the wind was blowing, it got cold, it rained, it stopped raining; you went away, my heart broke, you came back and my heart was okay. I think basically that is deep down what everybody wants to hear—it's been proven by numbers.

"So you start to think about the performer's role as an entertainer, and that the audience is paying money to come there and see you do something that will basically gratify them. And I have a conflict where I believe that people are entitled to get off as much as they can, and I think entertainers ought to do just that; however, I don't merely want to go out there and bullshit my way through a show. I want some substance too, so I have to mix it up a little bit and do some of the things that people wish to have done before their very eyes on stage, and at the same time keep myself from going crazy by writing down some of the things I want to hear.

"Usually after I finish writing a song, that's it. It doesn't belong to me anymore. When I'm working on a song it takes weeks and weeks to finish and the orchestra stuff takes even longer than that. It's like working on a construction of an airplane. One week you're a riveter, or you're putting the wiring in, or something like that. It's just a job you do and then you go onto the next step, which is learning how to perform it or teaching it to somebody else. I feel that all the material I've written, as far as my own appreciation of it, goes through a cycle where, especially if it's something I'm going to record, where you work on it so much that by the time you finish it you can't stand it anymore. You know, you just get saturated with it. When you get to hear it played right for the first couple of times, that's the get-off. After that I don't like it again until it's a few years old and it's been recorded and I'll pick up the record and I'll say: 'That's hip.'

" 'Brain Police,' was a phenomena because I was just sitting in the kitchen at the Bellevue Avenue house and I was working on 'Oh No, I Don't Believe It,' which didn't have lyrics at the time . . . and I heard, it was just like there was somebody standing over my shoulder telling me those lyrics and it was really weird. I looked around . . . I mean, it wasn't like 'hey Frank, listen to this . . .' but it was there. So I just wrote it down and figured the proper setting for it."

I remarked that Zappa seemed to be drifting away from the kind of social protest that characterized his early albums.

"I haven't become less conscious, it's just that I don't feel a driving need to write songs that are so obvious to everybody. We have one in the show now that's obvious to everybody, with some Richard Nixon jive in it. But I'd rather write 'Penguin In Bondage.' My experiences have changed, they're getting less specific in certain ways, more specific in others.

"It used to be that I would write specific things about obvious social phenomena that a large number of people could identify with because they had seen it in action. But that's less specific in terms of my own personal experience. You know, I could observe something happen that may or may not have happened to me personally, and I could still write about it. These days such weird things have happened to me as a person that I'd rather put some of those down and do it that way. That's why I have songs like 'Penguin In Bondage' and 'Montana.' I write about the things that are part of my personal experience."

"Montana," which is, in part, about a man who dreams of raising dental floss on a ranch in Montana, started out this way:

"I got up one day, looked at a box of dental floss and said, hmmmm. I assumed that nobody had done the same thing and I felt it was my duty as an observer of floss to express my relationship to the package. So I went downstairs and I sat at the typewriter and I wrote a song about it. I've never been to Montana, but I understand there's only 450,000 people in the whole state. It has a lot of things going for it, plenty of space for the production of dental floss . . . and the idea of traveling along the empty wasteland with a very short horse and a very large tweezer, grabbing the dental floss sprout as it pooches up from the bush . . . grabbing it with your tweezers and towing it all the way back to the bunkhouse . . . would be something good to imagine."

I asked how extensively he revised.

"Sometimes I show the lyrics to my wife, or after a while I'll get her to read them to me so I can see what the sounds are like, because part of the texts are put together phonetically as well as what the information is supposed to be. I change lyrics all the time. A lot of them get changed by accident. Somebody will read them wrong and it'll sound so funny I'll leave it wrong.

"I've always hated poetry quite a bit. I really hate it. The whole idea of it just makes me gag. And usually people who produce it—I don't like to make sociological generalizations, but that's not something I readily identify with . . . the suffering and the pumping on the chest with the closed fist, bowing of the head . . . leaves falling off the trees, the wind coming up and all that shit. I hate it.

"I don't like books. I very seldom read. My wife and I have a joke because she likes to read. I say there's two things wrong with the world today, one of them is the writers and the other is the readers. The main thing wrong with writers is that they're dealing with something that is almost obsolete, but they don't know it yet—which is language. Language as a by-product of the technological growth of civilization has . . . well, think of what's happened to the English language as a result of advertising sloganism. The meanings of words have been corrupted to the point where, from a semanticists point of view, how can you convey an accurate piece of information with this language?

"I'm not saying writers should be replaced. I feel sorry for them. They have a problem similar to people who write music. It's just as hard to write an accurate musical concept down on a piece of paper because of the new techniques on all instruments.

"The other problem is that I'm not much of a singer and most of the vocal stuff we put out I've had to give to other people to sing if I wanted to get a listenable performance out of it . . . consequently, if they don't say the things with the right inflections, it changes the meaning.

"There's just bunches of problems in getting the true meaning across. The only guy who's really got it made is a painter. All he's got to worry about is whether his colors are going to fade or whether his canvas is properly stretched because there's no middle man. He does it and that's it. He doesn't have to send it through a bunch of other processors.

"I think, ideally, the way it should be is you could use words for amusement purposes only, because the spoken word, the sound of words . . . strikes me as funny, because of the differences in people's noise-producing mechanisms. But as far as the information communicated in the words, it would be better if people could communicate telepathically.

"Actually, that's all a bunch of crap. Who needs to worry about all that technical stuff? I'm telling you, folks, I just don't read very much. I don't like books too much. I don't like poetry at all. And that's it."

Picking up an earlier thread, I asked Zappa if he didn't think it was the artist's responsibility to educate those who know less than he does. He didn't.

"It's hard for people to imagine that somebody else knows something they don't know. And suppose you actually do know something that somebody else doesn't know and you want to tell them about it, well, you've got a problem, because, first of all, they don't want to know; and if it's you saying: 'If you knew this you might be better off,' then you have to sit there and say to yourself, do I really want to tell them that, will it make them feel better, will it do them any good if they know?

"I realistically look at it this way. It doesn't work. I think that it's quite possible that what I have to say is useful only to very few people and I should not bust my ass to make it available to a large number of people, because, first of all, they can't use it; second of all, they probably don't need it; and third of all, I know they don't want it. So kiss it off . . . and boogie!"

Why then, I continued, would an artist keep making records?

"I think in contemporary America most artists try to make records so that they can eat."

Finally, I started clutching at straws. Didn't you ever have something you said get through to someone else in a positive way, I asked.

"Yes."

And how did you feel?

"All I knew was that I was tired."

ROBERT HUNTER

Robert Hunter is the resident lyricist for the Grateful Dead, rock eminences of the San Francisco scene. An underground poet with a solo album, *Tales of the Great Rum-runners,* Hunter has toiled largely in the shadows of the subculture, charting its frantic course with his lyrics. Lyrics which, by and large, have escaped the approval of the Top Ten chart.

Of special interest is the fact that this interview took place totally through the mails, with Hunter responding to my request for an interview with a ten-page letter. A second letter followed in response to my request for further information about the Aquarian Age and the dawning of same in San Francisco.

"I think one of the major significant points about early S.F. music lay in the traditional orientation of the musicians. Just about everyone hit rock music via an extensive folk background. Jorma Kaukonen was somewhat legendary as an incredible fingerpicking guitarist from San Jose. David Freiberg of Quicksilver had a folk duet [David & Michela] which I saw and enjoyed at the local club several times, and not till years later did I realize this fuzzy bass player was the same cat as the bearded folksinger I'd earlier enjoyed. David Nelson, of the New Riders, Garcia, of the Dead, and I had a pretty bouncing little bluegrass band called the Wildwood Boys and a good local following. Pete Albin of Big Brother and his brother Rodney always had a band together. This is a very sparse sampling of the characters who were around then and later, en toto, became the S.F. rock scene. It was all happening at once then, just as it will all happen at once again somewhere else, but not just yet.

"This is only the first thing that comes to mind about that scene. There are a dozen other ways to view it. I think the last big pre-media bash, was, in fact, the transition point from rural-America to media-America. As soon as the TV cameras screwed down on it the vampire began to drink and only those with self-contained blood units survived intact. It was ugly to watch the efficiency with which that scene was dismantled; 'The Abyssinians came down like wolves upon the fold,' there was no bone worth picking not stripped clean and the marrow sucked.

"The scene is just now getting back to normal, with a few casualties, and we find ourselves older but still directed. Those who made stars of themselves are beginning to look a bit sheepish about it, but most are big enough to overlook it. Music is still the real value and a cat who can play is still valued."

"Let's get back to the beginning then. The first thing I remember was my mother keeping me up to date on the pop tunes of the day. She was nineteen and played the radio all the time and sang the good ones to me while I bathed. At age three I knew the Top Ten and still remember most of them. I was pretty impressed with 'Ghost Riders In The Sky,' 'Tumbling Tumbleweeds,' and 'Dance Ballerina,' not to mention 'Don't Cry Joe,' 'Jumbalaya,' 'Slow Boat To China,' and 'Three Little Fishies.'

"And then along came Chuck. . . .

"There's three kinds of songs I mainly do: the ones I work hard at, the ones that pop out of my head finished, and then the jigsaw puzzles, where I carve lyrics to slip into prearranged holes in someone else's changes [collaboration].

"These are three different crafts, each of them has its own requisite talents, its rules and rewards. I am not so rewarded by the popular success of a tune as by whether I continue to think it's good. I'm not a hit writer. I don't know if I could be as I've scarcely tried. I try to give my work some endurance characteristics, aware that this is not what the market requires at the moment, but confidently expecting that what I do of value will emerge in retrospect.

"I keep to myself and don't have many associations with the R'n'R world; I fear it the way I fear Fame, Cocaine, Getting Rich, and Leading Others. Their destructive potential as a rule outweighs their gratifying aspects. I find a great deal of satisfaction in my writing, in the pleasant interplay of creative forces, and I spend a lot of my time with guitar, pencil, and cassette machine.

"I'm confident that some of my best work is ahead of me, some behind me.

"Songwriting as an art requires all the traditional artistic attitudes and disciplines: dedication, emulation of good models, patience, and resignation to the amount of acclaim allotted you (always seeming too small) as well as natural aptitude. Also needed is an unruly ego with which to do battle, so that your life is not empty of psychic battles and exploits—the raw material of mistakes. Without mistakes we don't learn *better*, and learning nothing better, have nothing to teach. Having nothing to teach we approach crafts empty-handed, with nothing to assert but identity, a questionable proposition to begin with.

"A good songwriter should be a classic example of something. I don't know of what I'm a bad example; perhaps that's a condition of being who I am. *Et tu?* An influential songwriter is a very paragon of what's to be avoided. David of Psalms may do for an instance. But even being a superior bad example is not enough without eloquence, and eloquence depends on whether your tongue curled to the left or the right at birth.

"A lyricist intent on exploring the heights and depths of his medium, who attempts to fathom its potential, must soon realize that he is walking a thin line between humility and colossal egotism. Making assured, positive statements to the world is a pretty presumptuous thing to do, especially if you know it will be heard. Though it must be done with caution, too much caution stiffens the art. Before that point is reached you must finally go ahead and trust instincts and hope they are pure. Many of us will be remembered as colossal asses and some recalled with gratitude and pleasure. What is written only to sell records, it is my expectation, will tend more to putting the perpetrator in the former category. Unless it's done with grace, of course, for I must grudgingly admit that pop is a craft in itself, though as much aligned with politics and demagogical savvy as with music.

"It was only in the last year or so that my work came under critical fire. For the first six years of my writing career my work was largely ignored or relegated to the rubbish heap of psychedelia, an attitude which brought me as close to throwing up my hands and quitting the work as I have ever come. Now I'm seeing the first direct references to my work. Being largely ignored has been as good for me as it has at times been frustrating. Now I am glad it developed that way: my work has had the opportunity to develop almost privately.

"To anyone contemplating entering this profession, I would extend my sincerest discouragement. It is a fiercely competitive field, a ladder with no bottom rungs and only a few top ones. Financially, you must learn to live in a state of imminent disaster. If money comes, it comes in a bomb, and when the smoke clears all that is left is taxes. This is by way of countering the myth that a songwriter's life is a laid-back Aeolian paradise. But then, when you get all that other stuff together and are still alive, it's a breeze. What isn't? At any rate, I'd rather be where I am, doing what I'm doing, than anything else I can think of, by which I judge I picked a suitable career.

"I've lately gotten into recording my own works and by the time this little essay is seen, shall either be enjoying some success from this endeavor or nursing my wounds. I'm into this not because of dissatisfaction with the interpretations of my friends, far from that, but because I am rather prolific, seeing that I put a great deal of time into what I do. This also affords me the luxury of more personal statements, as only I must be answerable for their content.

"I am loath to 'make it' on the basis of anything other than my lyrical work and rigorously eschew any avenue which might put the accent on my self, my life, or my predilections other than what is set forth in my work. If my reputation can be entirely founded on the quality, or lack of it, represented by my work I will be content. At this point in my career though, it becomes increasingly obvious that my work will not have the effect I intend if I don't sacrifice at least some part of my personal existence to it, other than what I spend experiencing and writing. Releasing my own record is a calculated gamble in this direction and I feel that I've attained sufficient stability to be able to handle the negative aspects of personal recognition with some grace. If this proves an ill-aspected trip, nothing much is lost but a trace of face, and I fully intend to continue my lyrical work.

"I'm living in London right now. I try not to drink or smoke as it messes with my creative frequencies, but so far have had only token successes. I am an extremist who epitomizes temperance as the crowning virtue and cannot by my nature ever quite achieve it.

"Now the sun suddenly comes through my window as it does every afternoon at three-thirty. It lasts until four-thirty and usually finds me in the full flush of my daily creative frenzy. It tapers off with the sun and ten to six or so will often find me unaware that the day has passed. I have to break for dinner and then try to take advantage of London a bit and go see something of interest. I live around the corner from the Victoria and Albert Museum, which I try to visit daily as a break in output to take some input.

"Everything is grist for the creative mill; anything which was done with grace, precision, and some consideration of the artist's place in the scheme of things. I choose especially, possibly perversely, things which have no great interest for me and try to develop an interest, as I feel that the areas of my ignorance are characterized by subjective antipathy. I spent several days, for example, studying examples of pre-reformation alabaster ecclesiastical decor. I studied it precisely because it was *not* interesting to me. I find, by exercising my facilities in such a way, that my appreciation for what *does* naturally interest me is greatly heightened.

"When I admire a poet I like to read his works into my cassette machine, then listen back, hoping to influence my work with internal music not necessarily my own. But it *is* my own when the work is finished, because I refuse to *incorporate* blocks of ideas while realizing the necessity of influence. In other words, I'm at a point in my career where I feel that I am faced with two alternatives: assimilate or perish.

"I don't see why work in the popular vein must be plebeian or obvious; with a bit of conscious effort it seems that all the available influences might be brought to bear, none more important than the others, but all crucial. It is my firm conviction that no medium is more apt to cover the territory, while remaining accessible, than the art of songwriting.

"My first song was written when I was seventeen [1958]. I had a rock band called The Crescents. I'm thirty-two now and my last song to date, as yet in the works, is called 'Jack O'Roses,' which runs into thirty verses and touches on most of what's concerning me at the moment. I've been working at it for about a month and a half and intend to record it here in London before heading back to the West Coast and the first order of priority in my peculiar scheme: the Grateful Dead.

"The Dead are the personification of my values in popular art. We began as traditional musicians, working in Old Time and Bluegrass music, were influenced by Phil Lesh to spread out and improvise a little, but never beyond capacity, and eventually, year by year, invented our own conception of the whole of the music native and accessible to us until it became something entirely itself. We never took day to day popular music as our guide anymore than we rejected it, and I feel that we have evolved a form of music which is not only unique but which gives each of us the ultimate creative liberty possible, short of license.

"If this should sound like blowing my own horn, I must add that I don't play or sing in the band but only write lyrics and never cease to be overwhelmed and entirely gratified at the context in which my words occur.

"When I was cautioning people against pursuing songwriting as a career, it was partially because of the rareness of opportunity when chance teams one with a group not only capable of interpretating his fullest voice, but so self-sufficient that they could most probably achieve close to the same effect (I hesitate to say undoubtedly) with the work of any other character who happened to be rampant at the moment.

"I mean, if you happen to be a writer and the geniuses fall by and ask for your help, don't say no because Hunter told you it was probably not a good idea and you wouldn't get far. If it happens to you and you pass it by while still feeling you would like to say something to your fellow mucksloppers, pass yourself up as too easily influenced."

JOHN SEBASTIAN

It is impossible to describe the feeling, being away from the Village for the first time, living in San Francisco in the summer of 1965, hearing "Do You Believe In Magic?" by John Sebastian and the Lovin' Spoonful as it rose up the charts toward the

number one spot. Hometown heroics! The local underground was being recognized out West, where it would take shape and return in 1967 to freak out the East.

John Sebastian's songs, finely polished gems of rock 'n' roll, today serve for a new generation of scholars the purpose that Chuck Berry's tunes did for John and his peers—examples of the pure form, on which to build a new one. His body of three-minute classics are what might be known to future generations as "Rock 'n' Roll circa 1966—New York City variety."

In 1974 Sebastian, like Dylan and few others, creates in the shadow of his immense past accomplishments. Surely an awesome task.

The interview took place at the home of his parents in Greenwich Village.

"I'd say the heaviest influence on my songwriting was approval. In other words, I was seventeen or eighteen and I wrote three songs. A band called the Mugwumps, which was a predecessor to the Spoonful, snapped one up. I recorded another one with a fellow by the name of Eric Jacobsen, who produced the Spoonful. And then about the fourth or fifth song was 'Do You Believe In Magic?' and the band *loved* that one.

"So this tremendous thing started. The only reason I was writing songs steadily was that there was nobody else writing songs in the group. It was totally one of those great surprises.

"I think in a way the Spoonful started off being sort of a jugband and country music influenced rock 'n' roll band searching for material among the various archives of great songs, and in the meantime I kept coming up with them. One time it would be a song; one time it would be an improvement on an old song. One time it would be 'Gee, this is a great melody, but they're never gonna buy "Colored man at the end of de war," ' you know, those strange lyrics that some of those old jugband tunes used to have. So that's when I started actually thinking of writing songs on purpose and putting time into it.

And since I never wrote more than, say, ten songs that didn't appear on a Spoonful album, you can judge my output totally by the Spoonful output.

"Whatever patterns that songwriters have, you can pretty much eliminate in my case. I've done everything from write a song in ten minutes to write two verses of a song and then five years later finally come up with a third verse. And all extremes in the middle. Many of the idea elements of the songs happened with me and Zolly throwing around a subject. Zol never liked to do anything like songwriting, so it would usually be an idea or an outgrowth of a conversation that I would then sit with and mull over by myself and try to come up with a structure. Then I'd sing it to somebody in the group who'd say, 'Gee, that's good, but did you forget the part when we were laughing about such and such?' And I'd say, 'Okay, we'll get to that in the third verse.' That kind of thing.

"My only standard was that I wanted to like the song, and I don't like very much. Also, I don't write music, so if I could remember it and like it, that was it."

Sounds simple doesn't it? But when you can turn out a magnificent string of rock 'n' roll pearls like Sebastian did during the mid-sixties, you can afford to be simple.

"I can say with no vanity that it was just heavenly to listen back to those early songs. The reason is, you haven't done it, it's not all you. It's, you know, modern miracles, combined with an awful lot of good chemistry that has to happen in the studio. Moments—you have to get a series of them. Magic moments that you did not plan, that you couldn't train for . . . that just happen. All of those things that have been thrown aside in the last couple of years as far as methods that guys adopt to go into the studio, those things all contribute.

"A forty-five is special. I mean it's three minutes of heaven. It's got to be an opiate. I never intentionally tried to write a hit, but some of them, maybe three-quarters of the way through I'd start to go . . . Hmmmm, and I could smell it. And listening back to the playback of something like 'You Didn't Have To Be So Nice,' the first couple of times, after we put the vocal parts on and the drum fills . . . it was, my God . . . something else!"

I asked him then if, during that time, he'd ever wanted to write something longer and possibly more personal than the small miracles he'd been creating.

"My writing was as personal as I wanted to get at the time. You see, I wasn't aspiring toward anything but what I was doing. I really wanted to be in *rock 'n' roll* and I wanted to write *rock 'n' roll* songs. If anything I was pooh-poohing people who were trying to put art into rock. At that time I was going 'Bullshit! That's really bullshit.' I still feel the same way, absolutely . . . except that my own horizons have expanded [laughing] to include a few more things.

"For instance, a song I spent a lot of time on recently is 'The Face of Appalachia,' about a young guy, thoughts occurring to a young guy growing up in New York City listening to country music. I knew very early on that it was never going to be a single, but it was nonetheless something that I wanted so much to get out and to have it done right, that I cut it five times before I was satisfied."

John finally did make the step out of the three-minute rock 'n' roll mold in a song called "The Four Of Us," which occupied an entire side on an album entitled, aptly, *The Four Of Us.* Covering approximately fifteen verses and three-thousand miles, the song is an autobiographical tale of a cross-country journey, written as it happened, week by week, verse by verse.

"That song was actually the outgrowth of Catherine and me, and for me it's very much of a personal love song. It was never intended as a million seller; I merely wanted, once again, to please myself . . . and the three other people on the trip. I also wanted to write something that was longer than three minutes, so I was very happy about what was coming out in that sense. During that particular trip I was writing all of the songs contained on the album. I wrote 'Lashes Larue,' in there and 'I Don't Want Nobody Else.' 'The Four Of Us' was just one of the songs . . . and it kept growing."

Although many people may not be aware of it, John Sebastian was one of the first of the generation's rock 'n' roll writers to make the great leap to Broadway, writing the words and music for a show starring Dustin Hoffman, entitled *Jimmy Shine.* John entered into the situation wanting to "put a rose on Broadway," but the way he described it, things were not so rosy.

"I told them I was writing songs for them. I had written half the songs already. Just by coincidence they fit in. I wrote one or two for the show, custom made, and they were so awful they were great. I mean what was funny about them was that they were making a slight parody of the desperation the lyricist always shows in plays. Very often you can see that lyricist up at three A.M. saying 'Christ, it's going into rehearsal tomorrow; I've got to have this done!' so that the words are just silly, you know?

"I wrote a tune for the show called *There's a Future in Fish, Mr. Shine,* which was my showtune. It was sung by the guy who used to play one of the uncles on the Molly Goldberg radio show.

"You see, they weren't sure whether to consider me important or not, because they weren't sure whether they wanted a musical. They wanted to have music in it, but they didn't want to spend the money to have music in it. So they were telling me, 'This isn't a musical, this is only a show with songs in it.' Okay, I got it. Then I'd say 'All right guys, you don't have to give me an orchestra or anything, all I need is a four-piece band.' And they'd say 'How about a three-piece band?'

"I mean, they didn't know where to put me. It was a bunch of people who were trying desperately to adjust to this new thing. They said '*Hair* made it; maybe we should pay attention to him.' It was so strange, and in a lot of ways I came to have such little regard for the whole style, the way the thing was being put together, that it gave me more confidence. You know, actors and actresses and directors relate to each other every bit as crazily as musicians. It's weird if you're not somehow initiated.

"Here's another thing they did. I had a song in there that they cut in half. The guy they assigned to me to teach the song to could not sing. Hence they said 'Okay, we'll cut the song in half and he'll sing half on his entrance and half on his exit.' So I said 'Okay guys, I'm just going to go ahead and make the record my way and make a recording of it.' The song is 'She's A Lady.' It's a nice song; it has impact on stage. It stops a show or two now and then in my shows. So I knew the song was valuable and I also knew that none of the people there saw the value, forget musical, the dramatic value of the song. So it was at that point that I, you know, became discouraged by the people around me."

Would he ever venture near Broadway again?

"Absolutely! I'm sure that something marvelous could be done on Broadway that could make everybody so much money that it would be fantastic. I would love to do it, but with somebody who had an idea or two."

While growing up John was subject to a wide variety of musical situations.

"I became interested in rock 'n' roll the minute I came back from Rome at the age of eleven. Allen Freed wasn't quite on yet, but you could hear an Elvis Presley tune. Then after Freed came on I became a rock 'n' roll junkie for a long time. But I wouldn't say that was the extent of my listening because I was listening to very often four and five hours of practicing a day— my father is a classical musician. Mom used to sing and she was always playing Ella Fitzgerald stuff and all the great ladies who sang in front of the big bands. I listened also to chamber music and the like. I was interested in these tapes that various friends of mine had, which was 'folk music'—this was far before it was fashionable. It was mostly sort of New York radical left people who had great tapes of various singers. Burl Ives was a friend of the family and he brought Woody Guthrie around for an evening or two, but I was a little bit too young to really remember that.

"Then, when I was fifteen or sixteen, I didn't want to hear rock 'n' roll anymore. I just wanted to follow Lightning Hopkins around and be the greatest living blues singer, sometime before my eighteenth birthday if possible. And also, during that period or before, I started listening to jugband music. And, of course, I was living on Washington Square West by that time, so I was influenced by second generation bluegrass.

"Chuck Berry's gotta be among my top three influences, but that's a cliché by now, to say you were influenced by Chuck Berry. I also liked the blues writers, like Arthur Crudup. I mean, whether or not it's the same musical format for eighteen verses, some of those verses were killers.

"I don't know if I was consciously interested in lyrics, but I do know all the words I've ever heard in a song. I have a photographic memory for words. Another thing I dug was being able to understand the lyrics . . . and on a lot of the records I was listening to, the lyrics were not readily understandable, so I would go to great lengths sometimes in slowing records down in order to get the words. Whether I was consciously saying 'This is great writing,' or 'I'll be a great writer someday,' or anything like that, it was nonetheless making an imprint."

I asked him if songwriters talk shop this way when they get together.

"I do it with a couple of guys, pretty much the ones whose lyrics I like. For instance, with Randy Newman, within the first ten minutes of talking to him we were talking about dry periods and he's so eloquent on the subject, and so hilarious. I love that guy. He's real cynical about songwriting, but Jesus Christ, he is so touching as a writer. And I never felt more sympathy when we were talking about dry periods than I did from him.

"The dry period I had wasn't in terms of not writing, it was just that I wasn't writing anything good. And my impulse when I'm not writing good things is not to release anything, which has not been the particular style of a lot of characters in the last couple of years. But now that I have a handful of songs I can't say I know any more about them than I would about any other batch.

"I've got a song called 'Friends Again,' a song called 'Stories We Could Tell,' that's a reminiscing song that I wrote for the Everly Brothers but sort of pertains to me and Catherine. But I couldn't tell you that I was changing directions or staying in the same place, because I always find out after the fact.

"Like I said, I've been writing when I was miserable; I've written when I was happy. I've written when I was unhappy in love; I've written when I was happy in love. I've written on the road, off the road; in a studio, not in a studio. So that even in the search, I couldn't really find a system."

Sebastian did, however, have a few definite statements to make about the process itself.

"As time goes on you start to like writing more and you start to become more conscious of it. I started wanting to write more and simultaneously to not write as much. In other words, there is a natural outburst that happens when somebody goes into songwriting in their late teen-age years the way I did. I hadn't done it before; I hadn't intended to do it. It was a wonderful thing that came falling out of the sky, so it was a very spontaneous, easy, and thoughtless process, not anything I worried about or particularly enjoyed going after. But I'd say that from then on I started to enjoy it more and to not have quite so much of a flood, which is only natural, because you write a given song about a given subject and that's one subject you can't ever touch again.

"It's not hard to write now, although it is harder than it was during my eighteenth year when I had never tried it before, when I knew something about rock 'n' roll that nobody else knew, or so it seemed. Now so much is just common knowledge; so much of the stuff that I've produced has already been copied by a second generation that it's hard to go into the same area that you've already touched and find much in the way of vegetation growing."

I had a final question about what seemed to me to be the growing ranks of people, now nearing thirty, who are currently defecting from rock 'n' roll. I wanted to know if he thought rock 'n' roll was something that people grew out of.

"I should hope so. Not that you grow out of it, but that it's out of proportion at one point in your life. I mean, at sixteen, when I think of how important songs on the radio were . . . you know, sort of awakening adolescent love combined with these certain chord changes and these great tunes—it was all one thing. So when Earl Grant came on the radio, you started to become aroused.

"Also, you're talking about the people who are now thirty. So you're talking about people who were twenty and under in the sixties, which was a time when the importance of music was so totally out of proportion, because everything else was so awful.

"A lot of things finally come up to replace it I think— families . . . real life. I think it's healthy."

FELICE AND BOUDLEAUX BRYANT

This husband and wife country songwriting team have been at it for more than twenty-five years, proving the old adage, the family that plays together, stays together. Their family of songs comprises perhaps the largest body of work in the field today.

Known internationally for their million sellers with Don and Phil Everly, the Bryants have written songs for such other

artists as Roy Clark, Bob Luman, Elvis Presley, Eddy Arnold, Charlie Pride, Carl Smith, and The Osbornes.

The interview with the Bryants took place at the Essex House Hotel in Manhattan where they were staying prior to delivering a lecture on songwriting as part of the 92nd St. YMHA Great Lyricist Series. Although it was a fancy hotel suite, during the course of the interview I felt as if I were a guest at the Bryant's own home, outside of Nashville.

Felice: "My writing was venting my feelings because I couldn't talk to my elders. I always wrote; I wrote letters and poetry that I would tear up so that they couldn't be found. I wrote all the time, even if it was only doodling. I had to have someone to talk to, so I talked to myself."

Boudleaux: "If I'm too close to a subject emotionally I don't like to write about it. I keep it to myself. I like to write though and if we write something I really enjoy I can get emotionally involved in it after it's done. But if I had a deep emotional experience I doubt seriously that I would try to set it to words."

A songwriting team, Felice and Boudleaux Bryant: a team of opposites merging each other's writing strengths into a hit combination. Felice, emotional; Boudleaux, realistic—he writes to live, she lives to write. But, of course, not quite so simple.

Boudleaux: "We work in many, many ways. Sometimes the lyrics come first, sometimes the melodies come first. Sometimes we work together and sometimes we work separately. Most of the time we work together."

Felice: "For a long time I had these ideas, but I couldn't tell anything about them while they were in my head, so I'd have to write them out, the words. I don't read music. I don't play an instrument. The words themselves will have a musical value. That's how I can compose a melody. Then he'll write the music down, or I'll turn on the tape machine. It's only then that I can evaluate the idea."

At the start Felice sang at amateur shows, usually coming in second or tied for first. Boudleaux was a professional musician, playing everything from country music to society swing. After they were married they moved to Moultrie, Georgia, where they began writing songs for fun, seriously.

Boudleaux: "We started writing for the hell of it, for fun, and after we had about eighty songs we thought, this looks like it could be a good thing. But we originally wrote them for our own amusement and we'd show them to our friends."

Felice: "Some people cut stones and polish them. We wrote songs. The family used to say 'Oh, ain't that *good*. Just listen, that's a neat song.' They were encouraging like you are to a child. 'That's nice honey, now go to your room.'"

Boudleaux: "They enjoyed the songs, but they didn't have any more idea than we did about how to get through the closed door."

Felice: "We didn't look for the door. Then all of a sudden I said to Boudleaux, I said, we're not fantastic, but we're not bad. Let's do something with them. And that's when he started writing letters."

Boudleaux: "I wrote about twenty letters a day to everybody I could think of, people I had known, people I didn't know. We'd get names and addresses out of *Billboard* magazine. We sent songs out all over the world for a couple of years without any results except rejections and unopened returns."

Felice: "My heart would crack with every rejection. I thought, well maybe we're not that good, because I was counting on the fact that the powers that be really knew, cause if they didn't know they wouldn't be there. I didn't realize that it's all guesswork in their department too. But it would antagonize Boudleaux when people would say, this isn't structured properly. I mean their criticism was strictly their own opinion. You don't come up to Boudleaux and say 'Man, you don't know what you're doing.'"

Boudleaux: "I'd been in the music business long enough to know they weren't lousy songs."

Felice: "He hangs his teeth and stays in there."

Boudleaux: "Some of those early songs were good and some weren't. The same thing is true for the songs we write now. You don't ever really know for an absolute fact that a song is rotten. Occasionally you make a judgment from a personal taste standpoint, but I think every song we write—that we finish—is crafted fairly well, some better than others of course, but you can't make any kind of absolute judgment as to whether a song is good or bad. Some of the ones that we ourselves have liked personally the least have been songs that other people have flipped out on, and some of them have been pretty good hits. And some songs that we absolutely just were crazy about and loved and thought were just the best we'd ever written didn't do a thing, and we still have them sitting around."

Felice: "And there's still magic connected with them. Until somebody else feels that same magic those songs will stay in the book. We have some songs on the books that are twenty-five years old, and still, when we do them the magic is there, for us anyway."

Boudleaux: "People come to our house to listen to songs and we bring out the books. We write in five-hundred-page legal ledgers, and we'll go through songs at random."

Felice: "People want to see our old songs because they want to see what the years of experience have done to us."

Boudleaux: "What they really hope to do is stumble across a good song that's been overlooked, because each person who listens to a song has his own idea about what constitutes a good song. One of our biggest songs was shown over thirty times before it was ever cut and that was 'Bye Bye Love.' It was even shown the very morning of the same day the Everly Brothers heard it in the afternoon. It was shown that morning and turned down and the fella said, 'Why don't you show me a good *strong* song? So . . . nobody really knows what a good song is."

In 1949, however, somebody recognized a good song when they heard one, as written by the Bryants.

Boudleaux: "There was a fellow I had worked with in Detroit, Rome Johnson, who had gotten on record as a country singer and we showed him a few of our songs and he flipped out on one of them, said he wanted to do it and he called Fred Rose of Nashville and told him about the song and we sent the song to Fred Rose. As a result of this conversation, Fred Rose didn't let Rome do it, but had Little Jimmy Dickens do it and it was a smash country record, just a stone smash and that's all there was to it. It was called 'Country Boy.' After about a year of traveling around we went to Nashville and started making contact with the various artists who were recording there. And from then on we've done nothing but write."

Felice: "At that time, in the field that we flopped into, the artists wrote and performed all of their own material. Then, after a while, the road got to them; they couldn't think, they couldn't doodle around on the front porch with a guitar, they couldn't stroll through the woods and get inspired. So Boudleaux and I were the first people who came to Nashville who didn't do anything but write. We were the factory—what an 'in' you know?"

Boudleaux: "There were many other writers in town, but they had to work at other things."

Felice: "We had to be very careful back then at what we wrote, because we could get almost anything and everything recorded."

Boudleaux: "There's one thing that happens after you've been writing and you're solidly into it, and that's that occasionally you will show a song that you don't particularly like yourself."

Felice: "And Boudleaux gets very angry because I'll say to the artist 'Well, I don't like that one.' "

Boudleaux: "I think that's a ridiculous remark to make to an artist, because it might have an effect, and the song could be ideal for the artist. I think you should keep an absolutely impartial attitude. Just let them react to it and if they react positively maybe you've got a pretty good chance. We had a song not long ago that we both thought would have been an absolute smash for Hank Snow, who hadn't then really had a smash in a long time. It was not the style of song he customarily does."

Felice: "Our song wasn't in the style he usually did, but it was his."

Boudleaux: "It wasn't the sort of thing Hank Snow's ever done, but it was the kind of thing I could hear in my mind being done by him, because he does have a very distinctive voice and this song was just the sort of thing that I thought would be an absolute total smash done in his way."

Felice: "Now there was magic that we felt that he didn't."

Boudleaux: "He didn't do the song and it still hasn't been done yet. But since that time he has had a number one country record, so I must acknowledge that he knows what he's doing."

Felice: "And we haven't thought of anybody to show the song to. The song just said 'Gimme to Hank!' "

Boudleaux: "Once in awhile you're able to bring a thing like that off. We had a song last year 'Come Live With Me.' The minute it was done I said that's a Roy Clark song, absolutely no way otherwise. It happened that "Hee Haw" was filming at the time and I got hold of Roy and showed it to him at the studio with fifteen secretaries sitting around typing. He couldn't hear it too well, so we went to a little cubbyhole office and I played it again . . . and he just fell out."

Felice: "He fell in love with a chord change."

Boudleaux: "It happened that his record producer was there and we showed it to him. They called a session just for the song, did it within a week and it was out a few weeks later. It went to number one."

Felice: "Whenever we've had this feeling and the artist has gone along, we've had a hit. And when the artist doesn't go along, that's so painful, because you can see it so clearly, like in a crystal ball."

Boudleaux: "We once high-pressured a guy into doing a song. The name of the song was 'Let's Think About Living,' and it was an all-out smash, but this cat hated it. Bob Luman hated that song."

Felice: "That was another one of those things that we saw that the artist didn't. We've had about five of them in twenty-five years. But in each song that is shown to an artist, you've got to remember his enthusiasm and you've got to remember that this is the hook he wants to hang on. If *you* looked at me and you said 'Felice, this is important to me. I have a heavy date and I want her to like me. I want to make an impression. Does this shirt look right?' By God, I'm gonna tell you what I think. I'm gonna say 'Blue would really work on you.' And if Boudleaux is peddling a red shirt that day he's gonna be madder than hell."

Boudleaux: "Because they might like red as well as they do blue, and they might look just as good in it. When it comes to songs I believe that you don't know if the song's good or not anymore than anyone else does. If it's crafted well, if the rhymes are true, if the thought is expressed in a fairly comprehensible way and the melody is singable, who knows, it might be the best song that ever came down the pike."

Felice: "I know, but the whole thing is, it only has cost us paper and pencil, which is nothing. Brown paper sacks we used to write on, and that costs nothing. But if you came to us and you had your sights on something, if I didn't believe in this paper bag here, I'd say 'Man, we've got one over there that might be better.' "

I stepped in at this point to ask Boudleaux to describe what makes a song a country song.

Boudleaux: "There are various kinds of limiters. By that I

mean a country limiter would be colloquialisms that are peculiar to say, the South or the Southwest, a rural atmosphere. It
doesn't necessarily mean the song won't be a national hit, but
it does definitely mean that it's a country song. It can be
identified as a country song, whereas some songs, even though
they are done as country songs by a country artist in the beginning, cannot actually be identified with any authority as
country songs because they don't have any limitations on them
whatsoever. A lot of songs that have these limiting qualities
about them just absolutely don't ever escape their limitations.
For example, if there's a song about chitlins and gravy and all
that sort of business, that song is not likely to break out and be
done by a pop artist.

"We've had songs ourselves that have been done as country,
as pop, and as rhythm and blues. There are a lot of R 'n' B
songs that are rhythm and blues only because of the interpretation that's given to them. Now if a record is R 'n' B only by
virtue of its interpretation then that song often is done by
country artists too. More often you'll find the transition goes
the other way. The song will start off as a country song."

I wanted to know how country music has been affected by
the changing times.

Boudleaux: "There's more permissiveness in sexual con-
notations."

Felice: "Kris Kristofferson brought the bedroom onto the
Opry stage."

Boudleaux: "We had one song that was banned on some
radio station because it had the word 'wiggle' in it. And we had a
song called 'Jackass Blues,' that was banned on all the stations."

Felice: "It's like a family. Did you ever notice that the
rest of the kids can get away with that thing and you can't?
Well Boudleaux and I still can't get away with anything suggestive. They've put a collar on Boudleaux and for some reason
they think we have no sex life."

Boudleaux: "We've got a lot of turndowns because there

was something maybe just a little suggestive, however 'Jackass Blues,' was written up by a famous columnist, Walter Winchell I think. He said it was the dirtiest record he ever heard. A few more papers picked up on his remark and it sold an enormous amount of records."

Felice: "That was our first *underground* record."

I then talked with Felice about certain technical problems of the trade.

Felice: "We save every scrap of paper, never throw anything away. We've got several ideas where there's just four lines and it's said right there; to stretch it would be wrong. It's not long enough to record; it's not anything. It's just a little whatever the hell it is and it's perfect.

"We had a title for years. Boudleaux's sister had a maid, twenty-three, twenty-four years ago. She worked like a dog but her husband sat home. She spent her life working hard and coming back home to this man who did nothing. When we asked her why she did it, she said the line; she said, 'O honey, I makes the livin' and that man makes the livin' worthwhile.' What an idea! What a title! And we have attacked that idea three or four times and never came up with anything that was as good as that title. And just to use a title and put trash around it is a sin.

"I had told this story so many times. The other night in Nashville we found out that the title of the new Roy Clark album is *I Make The Living And My Woman Makes The Living Worthwhile.* I have not heard the song but I'm dying to hear it to see what he did with it and will I like it, because that's the strongest title in the world and if you can't do it justice, leave it alone."

I asked if they worked every day.

Boudleaux: "We used to and we still do a little bit. We'll at least talk about something or maybe try to germinate some ideas. But we don't work as hard as we did."

Felice: "Well, if the pressure's on, if a request has been made and a session is coming up . . ."

Boudleaux: "We get a lot of requests from either the A 'n' R man or the artists themselves. The A 'n' R man might say 'I'm doing so and so in a couple of weeks; have you got anything?' And we'll check through our books and if we don't have anything that we think is what they're looking for, we'll try to write something. We've had a lot of success that way, actually. The material that we wrote for the Everly Brothers happened that way. The first song they did, 'Bye Bye Love,' had already been written, but then we had about five in a row that were multimillion sellers that we wrote specifically with them in mind. They weren't captive artists either. You know, they were looking at material all over the place. We just got lucky enough to have the songs that were absolutely ideal for them.

"I wouldn't just think of somebody and write the song for that person without having had some contact with the person, without the artist having asked for the song. In writing for specific artists you have to take a number of things into consideration. You have to know what their audience consists of. Whether or not they're appealing to a middle-aged group or a young group, young adults or teen-agers. And as nearly as possible if you can write a song that has a universal type of feel to it, you're in business.

"But generally, if you give a song to an artist and you don't know much about the artist's style, you know that there are many possible interpretations that could be given that song, so you're generally surprised one way or another, either pleasantly or otherwise."

Felice: "You've turned your child over to a couple of strangers and they have an idea of how to raise your kid and then all of a sudden here's this kid with a swollen belly, and you don't know how it got that way."

Boudleaux: "There's one thing I know that happens with us when we first finish a song. If we like it pretty well we'll sing it over and over. She'll do it. I'll do it. We'll do it together if it's harmonizable. And we'll do it till we're almost sick of it, then we'll put it away until we show it; we'll forget it, and after we show it and it's done and recorded, we just about totally forget it."

Felice: "It's fallen out of our Top Ten. The thing is, we have to erase the board to go onto the new song and not be hung up on the last thing. And when a song becomes a hit, something else takes over right then and there. You get the feeling that it isn't your song. It's your song till you put it out there on the street and then you've cut the cord, man, you've mopped its face with the apron for the last time. And when it's doing what it's doing, you don't even feel like you wrote it. Your name is there but it doesn't mean anything. All of a sudden it's not yours anymore."

I asked for a closing comment and Felice summed things up like this.

Felice: "John Loudermilk will tell you that he made a study of our material, trying to find out where the key was, and he found it, he said. And I said 'Yeah? Show it to me. What does it look like?' Because I still don't know what it is."

PART FIVE

Revolution/Pop
Strikes Back:
1966–1969

(Lash and
Backlash)

"Eight Miles High," by Clark, Crosby, and McGuinn, 1966

Nineteen sixty-six. A generation on the brink of freedom, dropping out at a speedy clip, unemployed, holding their breath against the draft, shacked-up out of wedlock, penniless, and stoned. Impossible futures. Incredible lifestyles. Vindication for the original seekers. Spirits soared under a constant diet of dope and rock music. Rock 'n' roll was still being played, of course, but only on AM radio. Rock, the music of the counter-culture, could be heard only on FM.

FM was in no way kid radio. It was youth-oriented *now* radio. In 1966, New York's first FM station for a short time that summer had no call letters, no newscasts, no time-checks, no weather reports . . . and no *disc jockeys!* Now the history of teen-age is jammed with the shouted inanities of some Uncle or Cousin or Father-in-Law Bob or Ernie, filling up every second of air-time with a continuous babble of words, the words themselves becoming part of the total sound. But when stoned you didn't need those words; in fact they became as absurd as they really were. So imagine the liberation of no deejays. This was adult radio in the best sense, not stodgy, but permissive, flowing, giving the listener some credit for a change. So what if you never found out any titles of the great songs you were hearing.

FM was progressive rock, song after song, sometimes for as long as fifteen minutes at a stretch—entire sides of albums! Songs whose titles you could only guess at, by groups you could never positively identify. Classics which would disappear from your radio waves forever unnamed . . . years later to turn up on debut albums by the Buffalo Springfield, Love, or Moby Grape.

This was radio that understood. It aided the feeling of communal solidarity that was building each day between the growing number of nameless longhairs occupying the streets. No matter what you didn't know about them, you knew they listened to FM radio . . . and for awhile that was enough. The underground ranks grew stronger while the legions of straights and squares stood trembling in their black (shiny) dancing shoes. (Just as a sidelight, the underground did away with dancing altogether, preferring to zonk out to the latest nineteen-minute Iron Butterfly drum solo.)

For the straight middle-class sons and daughters of the old guard a crisis arose—whether to drop out and join their ex-buddies in the underground, or stay straight and follow their fathers to retirement acres some forty years hence. At the same time fraternities and sororities and school sports dropped out of fashion on campus, as drugs and politics and rock took their place. Some well-known jocks knocked their professions in print and publicly admitted sampling dope (long before their preference for speed was made known).

So the system as it had been was in an uproar, with idols falling every morning. As previously-straights left to live on acquired savings, misappropriated tuition checks, government fellowships (in the form of Unemployment Insurance), or allowances from home, the thinning ranks of Clean Teens, barred from classes by students sitting in front of the doors, huddled together for comfort over milk and cookies, AM rock 'n' roll, and the growing distraction of television.

The backlash at this point was hardly powerful. It came in the form of a "Ballad Of The Green Berets," in response to an "I Ain't Marchin' Anymore." It came as a "Letter To My Teen-age Son," with a father telling his offspring that if he burns his draftcard he might as well burn his birth certificate too. It snuck in the backdoor via Merle Haggard with "Okie From Muskogee," informing long-haired America that the die-hard straight would fight all changes to the bitter end. Of course, no one in the underground took these songs seriously.

Radicals talked about getting guns; liberals wrote poems against the war; passives sat back stoned and drifted away on the dialog with the words of the new deejays Brother Ed and Daddy Love forming a lulling background. At least radio had changed . . . and maybe pretty soon the pot laws too, and the draft, and the war; why not? It was mind boggling to consider the potential power of the underground—especially when you were ripped on THC.

In its own way, this freaking out on the part of FM radio was similar to the mass freaking out on the part of its listeners. Freed from the limitations of the Top Ten and other vectors of public taste, FM played whatever it pleased, creating a beautiful chaos which exactly mirrored the times. But in the long run the numbers weren't as great as the predictions, and in order to survive FM had to give up its individuality and crawl back into the system through the delivery entrance with playlists and a Top Ten of its own. It finally became just like AM (which absorbed some of FM's tricks), featuring artists which felt at home on either band and whose records scored with straight and freak alike. Thus leading to the premature drying up of the underground's music as far as the media was concerned—one major casualty of the revolution.

In a similar way, the members of the generation, freed from the boundaries of a life based on the time-clock, the school-bell, the rising and the setting of the sun, experienced a peculiar reaction to timelessness after awhile that was neither liberating nor productive, nor even much fun; a dislocation which could only be alleviated by something tangible to do.

It was a question of stepping into a dream state where there were no rules, no laws, no commercials. As Bob Dylan has said, "To live outside the law you must be honest." Very few in the generation could handle that, for dope alone was not strong enough to erase the years of conditioning, the feeling of standing outside time and changes. After a long enough summer vacation, many pined for a way to get back inside again. It was at precisely this time that a new means of extending the trip arrived—LSD, the only way to fly.

"White Rabbit," by Grace Slick, 1967

Propagated by Tim Leary, immortalized by novelist Ken Kesey, LSD solved the problem of what to do on those interminable Tuesday afternoons that faced the dropout every day of the week. Where dope got you off for an hour or two, doubled your pleasure, doubled your fun, acid took you into another time zone—it wiped out the entire day. Once in flight there was no way you could handle your parents calling long distance from Peoria (or short distance from the next room). Sometimes even going on the street was out of the question. All those *people*, with such silly pointed heads. Who was that strange visitor from another planet, you or they?

The lines were drawn again. Some were able to easily ride their psyches out to the limits; others balked, fearing this step could truly derail their futures forever. Some who tried the drug emerged with new designs for living, turned away from materialism toward the symbolic East, a lifestyle of calmness and stillness, of doing less rather than more, charting inner progress rather than outer progress. But others never moved again, gobbled acid like candy and became trapped in the wonderlands of their own nightmares. It opened people up to the demons latent within them, the lure of mysticism, astrology, and the manipulation by assorted cult figures. Many people thought they could fly. Some tried it and failed.

While the Beatles saw it as a great tool for spreading love, Dylan's visions grew more shattering and desperate. What acid did was to reveal at last and beyond a doubt those tangents dreamed of in the days of "Yakety Yak." They had been there all along and were there right now; all you had to do was live them. That knowledge turned out to be too paralyzing for any but the very brave to act upon.

The Beatles with *Sergeant Pepper* were the love and acid champs. Lennon and McCartney had enough energy left over to branch out into subjects like fragmentation ("A Day In The Life"), spacelessness ("Strawberry Fields"), and the growing runaway rate ("She's Leaving Home"). But it was San Francisco that was the undisputed acid capital of the world, where a generation of runaways headed in the summer of 1967 (the Summer of

Love!) to the tune of John Phillips' "If You're Going To San Francisco (Wear Some Flowers In Your Hair)."

Both the Jefferson Airplane and the Grateful Dead (the two groups most consistently associated with San Francisco and acid/rock) had in common an unmistakable *acid ambience* which later came to characterize a generation: heavy-lidded eyes, a slow smile, long aching gaps between phrases and pseudo mystical shorthand language with knowing cryptic laugh affixed . . . the shuffling, unhurried gait. Nothing to hurry over.

Grace Slick advised feeding the head, finding somebody to love, and volunteering in service to community, togetherness—but not necessarily in that order. Politically, she seemed radical. The Grateful Dead didn't say much, but their music spoke volumes. Their lead guitarist, Jerry Garcia, in fact, with his prolonged philosophical silences, became a sort of spiritual guru of the tongue-tied. His message was simple: Let's Boogie! In L.A. Jim Morrison, resident poet of The Doors, implored us to break the barriers of consciousness and light our collective fires of sensuality. The generation tried to heed the literature constantly barraging it from every radio and bandstand.

The new breed of gypsies, runaways, tramps, and vagrants, most of them much younger than the original rock 'n' roll war-baby crew, were conspicuous that summer and summers to come in their absence of brains. To them LSD was the coolest thing since cigarettes and in some circles replaced sex as a way to prove yourself to the adult world. In still other circles it co-existed and served as a means of testing compatibility. Before sleeping together, two lovers took acid to see if one had been harboring any secret ill-feelings toward the other. On acid all was revealed, the super truth serum—if you could understand the symbols. Like, if your girl friend reminded you of an old sofa that meant something. It was best to admit it then and there . . . and perhaps see about having her reupholstered.

And then, when *Life* magazine got around to proclaiming LSD joyous fun, the backlash bit. Medical reports. Something about chromosomes. Leary got busted. Kesey fled to Mexico. The criminal element moved in, riddling acid with speed. Reliable dealers went out of business, left town. Soon it wasn't even chic to drop acid. The media cooled it as news and gradually people lost interest.

Except that in the seventies old acid heads can be seen wandering aimlessly, not quite able to catch up with the fickle drift of public taste, their heads hopelessly out of whack, expanded beyond all limits.

The acid-orientation seemed also to be in part responsible for the large number of religious converts who appeared, chanting, as the seventies rose over the continent. This was evidenced on the charts with "Spirit In The Sky," "Jesus Is Just Alright," "Instant Karma," and a host of other tunes in the "Jesus/rock" bag . . . culminating perhaps or merely continuing on Broadway with *Jesus Christ, Superstar* and *Godspell* (examples with *Hair!* of the ill-advised and ill-carried out "rock/musical" phase of the late-sixties—although I will say that *Hair!* provided at least a half dozen hit songs).

"Words of Love," by John Phillips, 1966

The folk-music dreamgirl became the new freaked out ideal of the rock generation—the hippie chick. Even before most aspiring Bohemians had toked their first joint, had written their first folk song, these girls from the old neighborhood, onetime classmates, were already there. Stories floated back about a certain Jo-ann now living in sin or in the Village. Diana, that fine and wispy thing, third row first seat, now smoked illegal weed and balled rock stars. Peggy Sue worked nights as a coffeehouse waitress.

This was the girl from Eric Anderson's "Come To My Bedside," after she'd kicked Eric out of bed. The lady from Mick Jagger's "Let's Spend The Night Together," the morning after, with John Hammond playing the role of the television repairman. Not only were these women tough and sexy and

cynical—nineteen going on forty—who swore like lady marines, chain-smoked Chesterfield regulars, and drank muscatel
from the bottle without even wiping off the top . . . but they
were also *deep*, privy to verities of life the average joker had
never contemplated. Sure, he had the draft, equal rights, peace
on earth to keep him occupied; but she had her damaged ego,
misplaced father-figures, self-destructive streak . . . the death
wish! Concepts it would take us years to grow into, much less
understand.

In "Suzanne," by Leonard Cohen, she was seen as a mystical
waif, dressed in the latest Salvation Army styles, who tempts
him with her kinky neuroses. To Bob Dylan she was a sad-eyed
lady, capable of anything, understanding everything, who
"knows too much to argue or to judge." Mick Jagger called her
"Ruby Tuesday," an illusive free spirit, as light as the wind
and just as breathless. The Beatles described her as "Lady
Madonna," beset by worries and children but essentially in-
spirational.

Once again the game plan between the sexes was subject to
massive alterations. Many a slow-paced Joe was forced to the
sidelines to sit out the sixties and hope for a change in the
next generation. Those who were able to dig the scene arrived
at Ruby Tuesday's place, suitcase in hand, and split a few
weeks later under the guise of going out for a midnight pint of
Thunderbird.

Sexually, the revolution proceeded no-holds-barred. The pill,
ban the bra, one-night affairs—free experimentation, free sex,
free choice. Then the see-through blouse, the micro-mini, the
X-rated film. *Playboy* magazine invented pubic hair! The
ancient art of voyeurism became the nation's new number one
spectator sport.

High on the sensual rush of the music, sensual legs ascending
the crosstown bus, sensual dope in the system—cascading stimuli
breaking through accumulated years of repression. Life inside
the pleasure dome was never lovelier. Even Middle America

got into the act with wife-swapping, nude encounter groups, strip poker.

By this time the original liberated woman, the folk-music dreamgirl cum hippie chick, had been sacrificed to the revolution, burned out on speed and deserted by one too many rockstar studs. She became the leader of the radical anti-sex brigade which arose in the night to bump men out of bed and reclaim a portion of their rightful share.

When Helen Reddy sang of invincible women in "I Am Woman," the message was by and large passé. Those for whom it struck home were the everyday housewives, the repressed legions—married at nineteen, elderly at thirty, up to their elbows in soapsuds somewhere out in the stricken midlands of America. They found hope in the fantasy of the song, the dream of solidarity with sisters everywhere. For others no hope was to be found in the literature of rock music. They limped from broken relationship to analyst's couch to T-group in search of identity.

"Heroin," by Lou Reed, 1966

Even while the dream was unfolding, there was a dark side. Crowded together on the bandwagon were losers from every sort of lifestyle who sought, through the easy availability of drugs, to fade into the tumult of the moment. Many never returned from the sixties trip—victims either of acid, the war or their own efforts to avoid it, crippled by the awesome power of their delusions.

While the decade sped on relentlessly, many were left behind, unable to keep up the pace, at the same time permanently knocked off a pace of their own. The seventies found these people somehow out of joint, trying to piece themselves together. The promise of the sixties left them deserted with no place to crash, no safe harbor in which to wait out the storm.

Lou Reed and the Velvet Underground sang of the dark

side, offered an air of perversion, unspeakable acts that were attractive to many; but this kind of self-destruction could be lived out only by a few. His songs, like "Chelsea Girls," "Heroin," "I'm Waiting For My Man," gave glimpses of a different region of the soul. A region which, in the sixties, many fell into in search of the ultimate high or the ultimate low. Unfortunately, many discovered those moments and never returned from them; the Andy Warhol superstars who died living out these subterranean fantasies.

By the seventies this kind of life-attitude, hardened, decadent, removed from feeling by the accumulated atrocities of the recent past, would be making advances into the mainstream of American existence. Kids of the sixties had seen their friends die from overdoses of heroin, space-out completely from too much acid, commit suicide emotionally and physically. They had themselves been gassed at demonstrations, maybe served some time in the local jailhouse. The easy middle-class way no longer existed for them. Their actions had gone down on their records and nothing could be erased. This was the price they paid for their freedom.

"Different Strokes For Different Folks," Sly Stone, 1968
The black man in the late-sixties found his image doing a one-hundred and eighty degree turn. He had started out in the mid-fifties as a feared alien, went on to symbolic underdog status with the coming of the Civil Rights movement, became partner in rebellion with the hippies of the early sixties, and found himself as the decade moved to a finish as the new sex symbol of the Woodstock Generation, revered for his stylish clothes, his natural rhythm, and because his "soul had been psychedelicized."

There was Jimi Hendrix with his flamboyant sexual image and his throbbing guitar. Sly Stone and his wide hat. Isaac Hayes and his gleaming shaven skull. Stevie Wonder got adopted by the jet set. Flip Wilson got his own show on TV.

Of course, by 1970, the circle would come full again, the black man being connected, rightly or wrongly, to crime in the streets—an object of fear once more.

"When The Music's Over," by Jim Morrison, 1967
When Jim Morrison asked the generation when they wanted the world, the answer he got back was NOW and the answer he shouted back to them was NOW!!! Fortunately or unfortunately as the case may be, he was to be denied his dream and the generation denied their world.

After taking over the radio waves, the college campuses, giving flowers to the cops, razing Newport, advancing from "Dancing In The Streets"" to "Street Fighting Man," halting the bombing and jarring a president loose, the rock 'n' roll kids got a little stoned on their own power. They thought they could get their man elected.

Although the hippie had been officially pronounced dead (at simultaneous wakes in New York and San Francisco) his spirit was on the rampage on the streets of Chicago in 1968. End the war, stop Nixon, bring the boys home from Canada. We want the world and we want it NOW! Those were the goals that brought them all together, one last protest parade for keeps. Here were your acid freaks, your Berkeley free-speechers gotten clean for Gene, your San Francisco dayglo sun-goddesses wearing Bobby Kennedy buttons; the folksingers, the idealists, even some old-timers, rising up together as one. And they were stopped in their tracks, routed.

Bobby Kennedy went down in L.A. just as he'd reached the crest of the hill. Gene McCarthy wilted in the convention room and Hubert was selected, bathed in the blood of Grant Park.

A haze settled over events, and a gloom descended on the day the election results were made official. The unthinkable had happened. It was too soon to plan another move; the defeat too bitter to contemplate renewal of the battle. The weary troops staggered home to heal and forget.

After consideration, the first reaction was to escape: leave the city for the country, leave the country for Europe or Canada, leave the world via hard drugs. There seemed to be a universal dimming of creative lights, perhaps symbolized by the emergence of the Archies (a rock 'n' roll group composed of no visible humans) who gave us "Sugar, Sugar," surely a placebo, which sold about ten million copies.

On FM those old friends who were still at the well delivered through their songs a despairing message: Paul Simon stranded on the turnpike wondering where his country had let him down ("America"), Laura Nyro leaving the world of music entirely on a train of tragic visions and hard drugs ("Been On A Train"), Jackson Browne mourning an acid casualty of the sixties ("Adam's Song"), Robert Hunter, voice of the Grateful Dead, describing a life lived on reds, vitamin C, and Cocaine ("Truckin' ").

It took until mid-1969 for the generation to reassert its lifeforce, to gather itself together one more time, a reunion on a grand scale for all the survivors, up in the country, upstate New York, a festival of love and peace . . . concepts already irrevocably out-of-date.

MELVIN VAN PEEBLES

The first major black lyricist who comes to mind, circa 1955, is Chuck Berry. To many, Berry *is* rock 'n' roll. His lyrics, however, spoke of a *teen-age* rather than an ethnic experience.

In the early sixties Eddie Holland (of the Holland–Dozier–Holland Motown combine) started churning out machine-like hits for such groups as the Supremes and the Four Tops. Smokey Robinson brought the process a step further, adding lushness and a touch of poetry. And David Porter (with Isaac

Hayes) provided stiff Top Forty competition from Memphis via Otis Redding and Sam and Dave. But still, aside from the performance, most of these songs could have been interpreted, identified with, even *written* by songwriters of any number of colors, creeds, and national origins.

In the late sixties Sly Stone represented the freakout of black lyricism, while Bill Withers and Gamble and Huff brought things back on course—in line with the rest of pop history. In the seventies, Curtis Mayfield injected a wordy prose into the rather sparsely populated field of black social protest (along with Whitfield and Strong of the Temptations). They were, still, more social than black.

Of all the black lyricists writing today, the one who perhaps most truly seems to be operating within the structure of a black voice, telling of a specifically black experience, is playwright, filmmaker, novelist, composer Melvin Van Peebles.

Author of two Broadway musicals (which between them collected nine Tony Award nominations), a movie script or three, eight books, and songs for six albums, Van Peebles has come up against a variety of reactions to his singularly unique style of writing and singing. Not all of which have been hostile. And although his songs have yet to gain Top Forty acceptance, his artistry, in certain elite, tasteful circles, continues to impress.

Van Peebles expressed surprise when I asked him to be included in this collection. Nevertheless he agreed to the interview if I could be at his New York office within the hour. I was there in fifteen minutes.

"I can't read or write music. I can't even play piano. I prefer to get a lyrical idea, or a story that I want to tell and then write it down. The idea usually comes first and then I sit down and find the music that goes directly along with it. The form, fast or slow, evolves afterward. And the chords come after that. Sometimes it will all come out fast. Usually I will have the form, then change words here and there a great many times.

"Right now I'm writing a play, I'm writing a novel, and I'm writing a film script. I find each stage of writing a different experience and each type of writing also. Songs are a gas to work on because you can hold them in one concept, and you can see where you're at, whereas with a novel you may have done fifty pages and you'll do another fifty pages and you're nowhere near knowing. Sometimes with a novel I'll do the overall concept of it and then fill in, sometimes I don't know what's going to be on the next page myself.

"Lyrics usually come as a spin-off. Because I do a lot of very heavy, long writing the music is a spin-off. It's not a release, but, having the discipline, say, of running the ten miles, all the time doing marathons, having to go around the stadium once is easy. And since you only have to go around once, I spend an exhorbitant amount of time on the lyrics . . . even though they may seem as though they just fell off. Sometimes I'll be writing one thing and stop to work on a song."

I asked him if he often got ideas for songs from certain lines of prose.

"I don't work from that end of the stick. I work from the other end of the stick. I'll write something and I'll say, gee, this is a film or a poem or this or that. I'll write a feeling, or analyze or conceptualize and then it dictates in itself the form that it's going to take."

I wondered what sort of feelings seemed to translate successfully into songs.

"Unfortunately it's very difficult for me to answer that, because I do not have the commercial success in songwriting as I do in the other things, so I don't think it warrants me giving an answer because I'm probably not adhering to some part of that form that I must, to make them work. They are succeeding, no doubt about it, but on a very limited basis. This enters into my mind only as a fervent hope that the songs will someday work. But if I change to make them work and if they become less than they were, then they're not working. I won't do it. I won't change them to make them less and end up being just what it was that I was coming away from."

What were his early feelings about rock 'n' roll?

"Well, I'd heard it, but I'd already heard the original from where it was stolen. And the music where it was stolen from in most cases had more validity. I grew up listening to Jimmy Rushing and the Daddies of the Howling Wolves and the Granddaddies of the Little Richards. I heard Dinah Washington before she had strings—which was cool too—but I knew her before. You see, all that changed with the advent of 'Blueberry Hill' by Fats Domino, because they used to have black records that were only shooting for that small, narrow margin, and when the universality came in, the larger money, growing up with the parallel cultures, the music branched out into those things and as it branched out the songs became bleached and homogenized and so forth, hoping for a shot at that market too. Probably one of the first historical examples that I can remember is Leadbelly, years and years and years ago doing 'Goodnight Irene, I'll get you in my dreams,' which became 'Goodnight Irene, I'll *see* you in my dreams.' Well, that type of thing happened, and something goes with each one of those chippings away.

"I've been very illiterate in my taste. Now let me explain what I mean by that. When I started in films I didn't know the names of directors. I'd just go 'Hmmm, yeah, well I dug that flick,' and so forth, and didn't ever realize the line that followed through. As far as I was concerned I was 100 percent consumer. I mean, when I heard a single, half the time I didn't know who was doing it, but I danced to everything. Also, quite interesting, I was influenced by the singers on the South Side of Chicago.

"You know, sometimes I'll get on stage and people will still look at my voice and so forth, but I'm not the least bit intimidated because the voices I remember hearing in my childhood sounded a great deal like I do—my first musical reality, you dig? Of course, there were other styles of singing too. Today it's all going toward one style of singing. And Blind Smokey, Reverend Skippy, these voices didn't have musicality, but that wasn't where that was headed from. And because of the programming of these things, many of the kids in the audience have not even heard those old voices. Now the Rolling Stones and the Beatles went back and heard these people and were able to branch out from there. Perhaps one of the difficulties with my music is that it doesn't explain itself well. Or maybe people are very provincial."

I wanted to know how he got involved with songs.

"I got into songs sideways, through the music that I needed for my films. When I did my first short film I needed music and I couldn't afford to pay anyone, so I had a kazoo and I hummed my soundtrack. That was 1957. I got into it parallel with my other activities. Then, in 1967 or 1968, when I came back to the States from Europe (I'd been gone for six and a half years) I was surprised to find that black music, lyrics-wise anyway, didn't really mirror any of the everyday aspirations, problems, or lifestyles that were going on. I mean, I felt the lyrics, especially in black music, had almost become just a phonetic accompaniment to the music; whereas you had guys, such as Dylan or Kristofferson, dealing with words, and even pop tunes had more significance—you no longer had the Leadbellys or Blind Lemon Jefferson.

"I think it's partly the form that can't handle it. The form that black music has now put itself into, the gradual limitation of one idea itself—baby don't go—and nothing else. I mean, you get the first idea and you get the beat and then you know if you're gonna shuffle or do the slop or the bump or whatever, and that's it. It's a vicious circle. It's attention span, also. You train people's attention span to one thing, in a very limited way, and they're much more easily controlled too.

"Now what I feel, in words, is that you can work with a thing that's indigenous to where it's coming from. It doesn't mean that it's exclusive to where it's coming from, but it's indigenous. So I conceived the idea of giving a voice—this is before Agnew was around—to the silent minority. That's what I tried to do in my original songs. Each song was meant to encompass a lifestyle, a personality, a character. What I had hoped was that the sketches, that my renditions, would be taken by mainstream artists and be performed in a more normal format. But it's never happened. That's probably been the most disappointing aspect of the whole musical part of my career. There's a lot of black groups out there, and none of them have ever chosen to do the tunes.

"It would be different if I felt that the tunes they've been doing had any significance, and I'm not talking about even necessarily revolutionary significance. You take most of the songs and look at the words without the music, and you're shocked with the intellectual level. They have one idea and a good punch line, which is cool, but that's as far as it goes.

"There are exceptions continually that break the rule, but I'm talking in general. There are some things the O'Jays have been doing—'Don't Call Me Brother' and like that. Fine. Terrific. Maybe it's moving a little. A lot of times I'll get notes that say 'Baby I dig this stuff; it's inspired me,' and so forth.

"What happened in *Don't Play Us Cheap* was that the music was for a specific show and for singers, real singers in the classical or pop classical sense of the word. So it was arranged differently. Now people will say 'Gee Mel, why don't you do it like that? Why don't you do tunes like that?' Well, the other tunes were like that, or at least that's how I heard it in my head. And I was all ready to say, if the Temptations asked me for one of the tunes, if they asked me to take a tune and arrange it in that format, I'd be more than happy to.

"I think there's just a general embarrassment on the part of the listener because I work in the vernacular. Not the bullshit vernacular of 'hey man,' but real vernacular, which doesn't seem as real to people . . . because it's too real."

I asked about working habits.

"I've got discipline, but because of the diversity of the work I do not have a particular discipline for music. If I had, tomorrow, a play where the music had to be done at a certain time, then whatever discipline was required, I'd sit down and do it. I have an overall discipline, the same kind of discipline that I could bring to an editing table for twenty hours . . . or doing four sets a night.

"There are certain places for me where I establish a sense of work. So you come into that room and you have that sense of work there. I like small, quiet rooms, preferably uncluttered. Overall conceptualization occurs late at night or in the wee hours. The rest of it whenever I can."

I asked if he worked easily.

"I hate it! You can tell I'm working now because the room is very clean. I've cleaned up the room. I've vacuumed. I've read the paper, sharpened 400 pencils."

We concluded by talking about the satisfaction to be derived from songwriting as a craft and art.

"The revelation I hope my songs bring to people about themselves, about the human condition, that's the joy. I had a very good experience recently at a prison. The prisoners really dug my songs. They were not intimidated by them. I started to do 'Lily Done The Zampoogi' and the prisoners all started clapping. They said 'We got a prisoner here who does that.' So we brought him up there onstage and it blew his mind. He had a band and everything. That's what it's about. And those guys became the family that now have done the play *Short Eyes*.

"It's very interesting that the kids who dig my work—mostly because I'm sort of a listening artist rather than a pop artist— are kids who had a theatrical background or a protest song background. By the way, isn't it interesting with all the protest songs that no black protest songs came out, or protest singers. I mean, there are two or three songs, but no real black protest singer ever rose out of that."

I asked Melvin Van Peebles why he thought that should be the case.

"Well, I can let you draw your own conclusions on that."

RANDY NEWMAN

Slowly but surely, almost against his will, Randy Newman has become a legend in his own time although not too many people know it, or his work. His legend is largely restricted to the hard core aficionados and a soft corps of music-business heavies who admire him unashamedly and re-release his notoriously poor-selling albums semi-annually.

Although only one Randy Newman lyric ("Mama Told Me Not To Come," sung by Three Dog Night) has hit the top of the pops, his lyrics—variously droll, poignant, and grotesque— have won the hearts of performers like Judy Collins; Blood, Sweat and Tears; Linda Rondstat; and Etta James. A noted hard-worker, Newman once had to be virtually pushed onstage to perform his own songs. Now the reverse is true. And surely the prayers of the nation are with him in his battles against the Muse and the rigors of the easy life.

Borrowing a quote I once used to describe the late poet John Berryman, I'd have to call Randy Newman the songwriting equivalent of a "cryptic critic in clipt verse."

The interview with the morose, self-deprecating Mr. Newman took place between sets backstage at the Cambridge Performance Center in Cambridge, Massachusetts.

"A lot of the people I write about are insensitive or a little crazy in a different way than I'm crazy. I don't ever actually run into any of these people on the street. Maybe there's a part of me in there sometimes, in what I'm having this person say, and my attitude is reflected in how I have him say it. Or like in dreams, you could say this comes from here and means that. But it's never a situation where I'm living through these twerps that I write about. Still, they're more interesting to me than heroic characters. Way more interesting.

"You see, *I* don't interest me, writing about me. I couldn't name you any song where I was writing about me. I mean there's a whole world of people and there's no reason why a songwriter should be limited anymore than a short story writer or a novelist. I hate songs like 'I've Got To Be Me.' That's an obvious example, but songs don't always have to be personalized.

"I've been trying to write something about a Southern industrial worker. I've had the idea for a long time. Stuff like that interests me, the average person, nothing startlingly dramatic. I read that they had figured out the average person in the country would be a forty-seven-year-old woman who's a machinist's wife outside of Dayton, Ohio. I wanted to do a song about her through this industrial worker character.

"At one point I was at this project fairly regularly and wrote a lot of songs real fast, but then I took a look at it and I didn't have a way to go dramatically. Parts were all right, but I think the songs were suffering because I was trying to fit them into a mold that couldn't hold them. Some of the songs were too obscure. Obscure to the point where people would say 'How great, how obscure'; but even if they did, that's wrong. I really don't like to do that to people too much. I would resent it if a fucking song made me feel dumb. And I didn't want to use anything like liner notes to explain it. I wanted it all to be within the body of the work.

"For instance, there was this fairly long song in there called 'Kingfish.' Now, that's what Huey Long was called, but who the fuck knows that? I was kind of interested in Huey Long— his biography. Someone wanted to do *All The King's Men,* but I didn't want to do it. When I was real little I lived in New Orleans. My father was in the army. My mother used to tell me about Huey Long.

"I still may do this concept. I do think a major work, a play or something, to make that try, would be more satisfying than getting hit after hit."

I asked Randy when he started writing songs.

"I was sixteen or seventeen. I was always going to be a musician. I never thought about being anything else. In fact, I never thought about it at all. My first songs were bad rock 'n' roll, typical Shirelles stuff. At the time I liked Carole King, Barry Mann, those type of writers. I liked the music better than the words, but it was a different time. When I started working for a publisher my only concern was that the lyrics should be commercial. We may have said 'What a great lyric!' but it was great because Little Peggy March could do it.

"A lot of people started out at the same company—Leon Russell, David Gates, Jackie DeShannon, P.J. Proby. Glen Campbell used to do the demos.

"I wrote lovesongs, whereas I'm not interested in doing that kind of song anymore. I think eventually I became too interested in words to put up with songs that said nothing, or in writing things that embarrassed me. At the time they didn't embarrass me, but I look back now and I would not be proud of them.

"But it hasn't gotten easier for me to write; it's gotten harder. It was easier when I was writing for people—not that they'd do it, but I'd have someone in mind and then I'd write the song and file it away and wouldn't have to think about it anymore. When I have to think about writing for myself, it's a different matter—what I'd be willing to put in Tom Jones' mouth and what I'd be willing to put in mine.

"In fact about a year ago I said to myself, 'I'm going to write a song for Tom Jones.' I was kind of worried that I was slipping out of the mainstream, or any stream. I didn't give him the song, but I did write it and it made me feel pretty good for awhile. It was a fairly representative Tom Jones song. Not a good one, just a representative one. I like being able to do things like that. Now all I have to do is be able to make songwriting seem less unpleasant, or I just won't write. It'll be all over. I'll have to go back to North Hollywood, or play in a lounge somewhere."

Randy Newman's attitude on songwriting is known throughout the music business. Also known is his penchant for dramatic overstatement.

"Everytime I've had to talk about this I've gone into a grim litany. I know I'm making it worse than it is, it can't be as bad as I think it is, but it depresses me just to think about it. For long periods of time I've been unwilling to do it, to be there all alone in a room. I don't mind if I'm all alone reading, but like when I'm walking into the room with the piano in it my legs begin to get heavy and I feel a pressure. Recently I've overcome my guilt about it, which had always acted as a goad. Now I don't feel bad about not writing at all.

"I don't know what it would take to get me writing again. I mean, I've had financial disasters, owed the government money. I had an album deadline looming over me. It loomed and went right by. Maybe in a way what I wanted more than money or sales or fame was praise, and I kind of got it. Now it seems I'm worried that I won't get it again, but it probably isn't as important to me as it was.

"When I was twenty-one I ran a Thermo-Fax machine. I liked that. There's a great gratification that comes with having a nine to five job, in that you had to be at a certain place at a certain time and you could go home at a certain time. You didn't have to impose any discipline on yourself. I wish I could get into a set routine. I've made up schedules for myself since I was eight years old, but I haven't followed one of them. Tolstoy made those kinds of lists for seventy years and never kept them."

I asked him to remember a time when he was writing and from that recollection to piece together some thoughts on his working process.

"I've always worked the same way. I just sit there. Very rarely, maybe a couple of times I've jumped out of bed with an inspiration. But usually it comes while I'm sitting at the piano. I hardly ever have the words first. A piece of a melody or a figure of some kind will be enough to get me going, and sometimes it'll be right there where you can see to the end of it. And sometimes it won't and you'll change it and you'll go somewhere different than where you thought."

I asked him why his songs are generally so short.

"I guess I just say what I have to say and that's all I have to say about it and I'm done. There're a couple of songs that could have been longer or more successful, like 'Beehive State'; I really couldn't think of anything there. I tried. But usually I'm just happy to be done. I can generally feel when they're finished. I've been wrong a few times, more than a few. I have urges to change them all the time. I would do it, but I know I could never get them right. There's ruin there if you start to do that. But I can't think of many of them where something musically or lyrically doesn't really bother me. Which is another deterrent from working. You bust your ass with a crazed kind of worrying about every little thing and then you wind up seeing all these bad things about it two weeks later. It's a psychosis. It can't be as bad as I think it is. In performing them they all seem okay. It's only when I have to think about them. . . .

"Performing is so easy, so immediately rewarding. Writing, although I know it's more important, is just rough. I had a talk with Nilsson once and I thought he was crazy. He said he didn't want to perform because he thought the audience would sway him unduly about songs and he might get to thinking shit wasn't shit and that something that was shit was okay. Now I'm not convinced that he was totally crazy. Or it might be that performing is so easy and lucrative that I'm getting the gratification that I used to only get through writing, without all the grief.

"Actually, I could quit *both* and just do nothing at all. I'm capable of doing absolutely nothing for long periods of time without much remorse. But every once in a while in the morning I'll wake up and say 'Jesus Christ, what a waste. What a big talent I used to be, like a meteor across the sky.' "

Does he like any of his songs?

"I still like 'Davy The Fat Boy'; I always liked that. I kinda like 'Political Science,' but I didn't like it for a long time. I thought it was too close to a Tom Lehrer-type song, not that there's anything wrong with Tom Lehrer. I'm proud I wrote 'Sail Away.'

"In fact, the thing that did precipitate some of my writing was the Watts riots of 1965. I think that's the biggest thing that happened, the biggest shock to me, and the biggest inequity in this country. The way black people are treated in this country is obviously the worst thing to me. I always felt that the race situation was worse here than anywhere.

"Other than that, I'm essentially apolitical. I don't think my views are of any interest. I never could buy the sincerity of all those people singing the peaced-out numbers, but I wouldn't quarrel with the sentiments."

At this point our conversation suddenly veered into a high-pitched reminiscence by Mr. Newman on the early days of rock 'n' roll.

"I remember the day I first heard of Elvis. Everyone was giggling and laughing at school saying 'What's an Elvis Presley?' I think I was in junior high. I liked some of his stuff. I liked 'Heartbreak Hotel,' and I liked the narration in 'Are You Lonesome Tonight?'

"I never could dance too well, but I was in a club and all at school and in a feeble way I was into it. I haven't seen anything recognizable in these films that are supposed to be so accurate. Some of *American Graffiti* maybe . . . but it was all more sullen and boring and small and vile. You know, barfing and stuff, making fun of ugly people. There wasn't any of that fairyland stuff that I've been seeing. It was social castes, where you ate your lunch, standing around looking tough . . . or whatever the fuck you were supposed to do.

"I went to my high school reunion. That was something! I remembered a lot of people. Jesus Christ it was tremendous. A lot of people had been beaten down by life. Some of the girls who looked tremendous in those days didn't look tremendous anymore, and others had come on a bit. And I discovered that everybody was scared all the time socially, whereas I thought that people were really together. Talking to them I found out they weren't together. No one was.

"There were very few freaks. It was all very middle of the road there, drinking and getting into trouble. Now, one guy, who was always going to be a farmer, freaked out in some way; it might have been acid. The least likely person you'd expect. He's a theater arts major. His brother had wanted to be a baseball player. Now he's selling sandals.

"It's a meaty topic, and nobody's done it right. Not the reunion business, but the whole way it was. I've thought about it for years. It was so seedy. You might have thought it was fun. I mean, at this reunion we talked about all the good times, how sick we were. But it was pretty grim and not for me alone. I was all right, you know, on the approved list. Although I never approved of the approved list.

"A little later on I was in a band. We were really terrible. It was a band started by this trumpet player. He had a trumpet with him all the time but he never played. He organized the band. We had our first thing at some fraternity party. I think I was still in high school. We got up to play. It was the first time we were ever going to hear him. And he fell off the bandstand and that was it. I think he fell off on purpose.

"I remember a dodgeball game, just me and one other guy left, and half the school was watching. I was in the third or fourth grade. And everyone was yelling and cheering and I finally got hit and everyone went crazy, carrying the other guy off. And I cried. . . .

"God, the torment! Ugly girls—go ask her to dance. What a great subject that is. Of course, I only remember the bad stuff."

LOUDON WAINRIGHT

Another of the new breed of songwriters—sharp, witty, terse, incisive—Loudon Wainwright III—arrived on the Greenwich Village scene just as it was fading from public view, and thereby perhaps missing out on some of the recognition he might easily have garnered had he timed his emergence a bit better. He was already into his third album before people began hailing him as an overnight flash.

His songs are mini-portraits of domestic life. By focusing his piercing gaze on the small, often overlooked, yet painfully real nuances of existence, Wainwright has enlarged our understanding of such subjects as nicotine addiction, marital relationships, and the arrival of a baby. On the other hand, not to be typecast, he has written about busting up his guitar, getting drunk, sport fanaticism, and dead skunks in the middle of the road, showing us a vision that is as diverse as it is sly as it is ludicrous.

His father is a prominent journalist, once associated with *Life* magazine. Loudon and his wife, Kate McGarrigle (a tal-

ented songwriter in her own right), broke precedent recently by naming their firstborn son Rufus.

The interview with Loudon Wainwright took place in the offices of Columbia Records.

"Like every other kid I had to write compositions in school and I wasn't particularly successful, from a grade point of view or a school point of view. Once I tried to write a play. Songs seem to be the easiest thing for me to do in writing. It's not easy; it's hard for me to do, or at least hard for me to get to that place where I'm saying, 'Whoosh, I'm doing it.' The idea of writing prose, or writing a book or a play, or even writing poems—although I haven't really tested myself—appears at this point to be beyond my ability.

"I've always wanted to be a performer. I really wanted to be an actor in the theater. When I started getting interested in the folk-music scene I went out and bought a guitar and I started to learn, bought Pete Seeger records and that whole trip. I started to build up an identity. But my acting identity kind of won out for awhile and I stopped concentrating on music. But I always put records on and mouthed-over words, stood in front of the mirror with my guitar and everything.

"The first song I wrote was a lousy song, but it was enough to excite me. 'Holy shit, here's something I've never done before!' I was living in this guy's house and I hadn't played the guitar for awhile—this was 1968. I wasn't doing anything; I was being like a hipster, just wandering, and this guy had a guitar in his house and, lo and behold, I remembered the chords and a song kind of popped out. It wasn't a very good song—I even knew it wasn't a very good song—but then I wrote another one and it appeared that maybe some of them were okay. And they got better and better and people began to say— you write songs."

I asked Loudon the age-old, which-comes-first question.

"In general I put the words down first. On occasion I have

done the opposite, or very occasionally simultaneously. But mostly I write the words and then I find a tune, because I'm not a musical head. I have a very limited knowledge of the piano. Usually I write songs quickly, that is to say in a period of three hours. Sometimes I can write a song in ten minutes. I'm less prolific now than I was at the start. But, especially with the editorial sense I've acquired, I'm more productive, because I dig what the final product is.

"It's hard for me to write because I'm very lazy. I have to be at the point where I feel something's happening. I don't sit in front of a typewriter, or with a pencil and paper and say 'Now I'm going to write a song.' I had to do that in school, in composition. If somebody says to me, 'You used to write a song a week, why don't you do that anymore?' I say, 'I haven't got the energy. I'm too caught up in the rest of this trip.' When I stopped working this summer I started writing songs again. I started getting interested in songs. It's not just a thing of saying, well I'm not working tonight so I can write a song. I have to get my head into a place, it might take a couple of days, and then all of a sudden . . . bang!

"A lot of these other writers collaborated, like Carole King and Gerry Goffin, Leiber and Stoller. I don't collaborate with anybody. I was speaking to Bernie Taupin—Elton John's lyricist—again, he's a collaborator. He apparently is incredibly prolific. We were talking about this very problem and he looked me in the eye and he said that he could write an album in two weeks. And he thought it would be possible for him to write the lyrics to twelve songs [he writes the lyrics and gives them to Elton John, and John puts the tunes to them] in *one day*. Now, it would be a sixteen-hour day, but he thinks it's within his power to knock them off one every hour or so. I'm not that way at all and I'm not sure I'd want to be. But I'm sure I'd be a lot happier if I could write a song a week, as opposed to a song a month, which is about my current rate—

which means that sometimes I'll write three songs in one month, and then not write another song for three months.

"I just wrote a song this summer that I spent an unusually long period of time on. It's called 'The Swimming Song,' and I had written the first verse of it two years ago but I had junked it. All of a sudden I saw a way to complete it. I have a couple of ideas now that I think would be fun to write about, but I haven't actually gotten down and written them—but they're still there."

Who does he look to primarily for editorial assistance?

"I have a manager and I have friends who have made suggestions, whether it's about a title or whether it's about a lyric or structure . . . and I listen to their criticism and I have taken their criticism—but it doesn't come up too much. I think, as far as myself goes, to a certain extent I've developed, as I said, an editorial sense which I've kind of grown to trust. I'm aware that it comes from a subjective place, so consequently it might not be as valid, but where I used to write a bunch of songs which I would consider to be dead wood, all of a sudden it appears this editorial sense is cutting down that ratio.

"For instance, I wrote three songs this summer [1973] and I wasn't working my ass off and I had lots of time, but I thought that the three songs were as good as any I've written.

"Of course you also have critics who criticize your records once they're out—but by then it's too late. I mean, you can use it for next time if it's constructive. There is such a thing as not constructive criticism. On a given particular song of mine people have said, 'This song is too cute, too clever. What he's doing here, instead of being incisive as he has been on other songs, he's only being cute.' That kind of hurt my feelings, but in a way I agreed with it. It's a song that works well in performance because you can be cute onstage and get away with it, but not on a record where you have to listen to it a whole bunch of times.

"So I'll play it for my wife or my manager and that's about it, unless I'm sure I know it's what I want it to be."

Loudon Wainwright's career began on the coffeehouse scene. Along with James Taylor and the Chapin Family, he defined the latter phase of Greenwich Village in the sixties just as in boom times Bob Dylan, Eric Andersen, and Phil Ochs had defined it before him.

"I played the Gaslight a lot. I shuttled between New York and Boston. The Gaslight that I experienced—there were people there who were exciting and good and there were exciting moments that I experienced. I played on bills with Van Ronk (but it wasn't in Van Ronk's heyday), Pat Sky, Carolyn Hester, people who were involved in that scene, but three or four years earlier, when I was still in boarding school.

"It was exciting for me to be playing at the Gaslight. I had friends who wrote great songs. There were fantastic nights at the Kettle of Fish. But it wasn't like a real scene. It wasn't like 1920s Paris, or like 1961 MacDougal Street. The Village was in a state of decline. The Gaslight had been in a state of decline and then Sam Hood (son of the original owner) came and got it back on its feet. He got good people in there like Jack Elliot and James Taylor.

"I mean when I was there it was initially just a horrible scene. I was playing third act and most of the people who were there were Japanese tourists. Here is the Village. This is Where It's At. It wasn't particularly exciting—but still, it was exciting to me because I was really idealistic and really hot to trot and to get up there and have people applaud me.

"And I would go up to Boston to play at clubs that also had heydays which were over too. Like I'd play the Unicorn. Now the Unicorn used to be a big Boston club. Even then, what was happening at the time was rock 'n' roll."

I asked him if he thought a scene like the sixties folk might surface today.

"It ain't gonna be the same. Just like there's no new Bob

Dylan—it's not gonna be the same. Too much has happened in between, and even if not that much had happened or if specific things hadn't happened, I don't think the Philadelphia Folk Festival or the Buffalo Folk Festival or the Mariposa Folk Festival are ever going to be the Newport Folk Festival. I used to go there and I'd hear Richard Fariña and Jack Elliot and Bob Dylan and the Kweskin Jugband, and I was knocked out by it and influenced by it. I mean I've played two years at the Philadelphia Folk Festival and I've enjoyed it. I enjoyed myself at Buffalo. And Steve Goodman and John Prine and Bonnie Raitt are great. But this generation, and I suppose I'm a member of it and it's important that we're writing songs, is just not the Newport Generation. It's never gonna be Newport 1961 again.

"Now there might be something else that could happen which would be different. I can't be objective because I'm involved in it. Maybe it'll be as good or as fruitful or as exciting or as stimulating, and maybe there will be a Paris 1920 somewhere. It might be in Austin, Texas. A lot of people are moving to Austin, Texas. They're saying something's happening down there.

"It's good that it's different now, I suppose. Rock 'n' roll is commercially king and people are doing different things. I mean you have somebody like Martin Mull, who comes on the stage with his living room furniture and plays. I mean, that's as good or better than a lot of things that happened in the sixties. People are writing in different viewpoints because so many other things have happened. So it's better and it's worse; more exciting, less exciting.

"But I relate more strongly to what happened at Newport in the early sixties (I'm part of a tradition to a certain extent) than I relate to Bill Haley and the Comets, or even the Beatles who were of my generation. I mean, I was buying their records and flipping out over them, but I didn't go out and buy an electric guitar and I wasn't in rock 'n' roll bands. My idols were the acoustic folk heroes, like Jack Elliot, who is still my idol. I think what he does is valid. I have his records and for me they still hold up, they're good and they're important, and I know a lot of other people who feel the same way. I mean there is a demand, an emotional demand for that kind of music.

"Like once after a concert in Texas the fifty-five-year-old janitor of the hall came up to me and he asked 'Did you really write that song?' ["Dead Skunk"] and I said 'Yeah.' And he said, 'I love that song so much, everytime I hear that song I jump up and down.' I think that's just great."

I asked Loudon about some of his other passions, aside from songwriting.

"I love to watch sports—the pennant races, the Stanley Cup, the Super Bowl. I had a television set up in my dressing room before my last show to watch those Mets–Pittsburgh games. And last night at Willie Mays Night I was in tears. Sports is really the most outfront form of entertainment there is. There's no punches pulled, if you'll excuse the expression. (I just saw the Muhammed Ali fight on closed circuit TV.) It's so dramatic and pure, the justice is so poetic.

"On my third album I have a song called 'Hometeam Crowd,' which is my favorite on the album. The lyrics go 'Seventh is the heaven, nine is the cloud, it's great to be one of the hometeam crowd. When the Lakers beat the Knicks in basketball, I beat my head against the wall. When the Bruins beat the Rangers for the Stanley Cup, I got so drunk I couldn't stand up. When the Mets didn't win I got upset. I got bullet holes in my TV set.'* It's a minute and a half song, but it's my favorite song on the whole record. I just love to go into bars and get drunk and watch. It's an esthetic, dramatic, powerful, artful thing."

I asked Loudon for his feeling on contemporary music.

---

* "Hometeam Crowd" by Loudon Wainwright III, © 1972 Frank Music Corp. Used by Permission.

"I'm interested in some of it and I like some of it, but I don't have a radio or anything like that. I have a record player and I play records and I buy records. I read *Rolling Stone* occasionally, but I don't really have a topknotch knowledge of what's happening. I respect John Prine. I think he writes very good songs. I think Randy Newman is a good songwriter. I love Ray Davies and I love the Kinks and I buy all their records.

"I do a little reading. The last book I read was the Kerouac biography. And I watch a lot of television, maybe it's because I don't have to work so hard at it. It gets my mind off everything."

What about writing for films or the theater?

"I have fantasies about it, but the desire is not strong enough at this point, so I'm not going to go in a hole and start writing plays or scenarios. I have a playwright friend and he and I were talking about it—anything is possible and I'm open to try a lot of things—but right now I'm expending large amounts of energy being a singer/songwriter the best way that I know how to do it."

The future plans of Loudon Wainwright?

"Taking everything into consideration, the fucking world could explode or I could lose my record contract, or I could get my hand chopped off in a car accident, but taking into consideration that I continue and can continue to make a living and that an audience will still be interested, I could see myself continuing for a number of years in this venue. But I can also feel the beginnings of different ideas, which we've talked about.

"Of course the possibility also exists that in another year at this time I'll be so freaked out by the music business and this whole scene and so bored and down—which I am occasionally —that I'll just want to go to Japan and become a recluse, or something equally ridiculous."

JOHN PRINE

Although at first he may sound like an early incarnation of Bob Dylan, lyrically John Prine has a voice all his own. Fusing his country and western background with a rock beat and folk sensibilities, Prine has succeeded in producing over a relatively short career, a body of work that is as powerful as it is eloquent. Plus, he's got a sense of humor.

His songs, which focus on life's little people, have drawn the praise and respect of everyone from Kris Kristofferson to Bette Midler, including Dylan himself. "Sam Stone," about a returning Vietnam soldier turned junkie, is a classic of the post-sixties period. Far from another protest song, it renders reality with imagery both shocking and profound.

The interview with John Prine took place at a restaurant in New York City. The usually shy and taciturn ex-postman warmed easily to the subject at hand, becoming quite verbose . . . sometime around the third drink.

"A lot of stuff has come out of just writing a couple of pages and rambling on, going from one mood right into another. Then I put it away and if I wait long enough I pull it back out and the good lines stay there and the others just fall right off the page. You can't tell the good lines from the bad lines right at first sometimes—it's a matter of editing. I happen to type at the same speed I edit, so a lot of times I can knock out stuff while I'm typing it.

"Once I had about three-quarters of a page that I got three songs out of. A stream of consciousness thing that didn't make any sense at all as it was. That's why I made it into three different songs. A lot of times I'll find a good line that I just can't use in the thing I'm working on, and rather than try to beat

it to death, I'll file it away and pick it up when it's fresh again. I've done that really often—gotten two songs out of one thing I've started on.

"I'm very sloppy about keeping papers straight. My wife tries to keep it all together, but I purposely leave it around because I like to surprise myself. I like to write stuff and forget about it and then find it again.

"Usually the best thing is a real, real strong line that's a strong image. Sometimes an entire song will pour right out after it, if it's real strong. In most of the ballad stuff I do I try to use a chorus like a needle and thread, to pull the song together. A lot of times I've written just with the idea of experimenting. 'Donald and Lydia'—I had no idea what I was going to write about, but I knew how I was going to set the song up. I was going to set it up character by character.

"In general I'd say it's not subjects I'm trying to pinpoint, it's different moods. I'm trying to find a situation that would fit the mood. I'm more interested in the framework. A lot of times I'll pick the form before I write the song, because otherwise you run out on too many tangents. If you happen to run out on a good tangent, fine . . . then you can start all over again with that. . . ."

I asked him if he constantly revises his songs or if he gets them done rather easily and moves to the next.

"A song's not finished until I consider that I'd do it for anybody. But when I finish it, right there and then it's certified. I've heard other writers give suggestions years later about changing a line or something, but once I finish a song—this is even before I record it—I figure it's like a book on a shelf. It's already done and I can't do anything about it.

"I do have a lot of stuff that's half finished. I've got a song that I've been working on for a year and a half. The first part of it came out in like three seconds—the first verse and chorus. I can't get any further than that and keep up with the original theme of it, so I have to keep going back to it until I get it right. I really hate to stop when I start with an original idea, because it's really hard to pick up on it again. It's possible, but it's real difficult.

" 'Mexican Home,' on the third album, took me two and a half years. I had to end up changing the melody in order to finish it. The old melody had been finished first and I couldn't fit the second half of the song into it, so I changed the entire melody and wrote new words for it. Of course, now I have the original melody for some new words, and it's a good one.

"When you hear somebody else do the song, that's when you get a chance to criticize lines that you wrote. Whenever I hear my own records, I know it's my voice. I'll end up listening to the arrangement. But when I hear it done by somebody else . . . sometimes it brings up lines I thought before were just a link between two other lines, and all of a sudden that line stands out, depending on how someone interprets the song."

John provided his own assessment of his songwriting talents.

"I think I'm a better lyricist than melody writer, so I'm trying to balance out the two, because what I'm doing is writing songs, I'm not writing stories and I shouldn't always let the story carry the thing. That's my main criticism of my own writing. I'm consciously trying to stay away from ballads.

"Remember when the comedians used to get up and recite Elvis and they'd try to make it sound stupid? It would always fall flat because of course the lyrics didn't mean anything without the music. Those were some of the greatest lyrics, very simple and basic, and they went exactly with the tune. I would like to be able to write that kind of lyric too."

We discussed early radio experiences.

"The people who made the biggest impression on me as lyricists were Hank Williams, Dylan, Roger Miller—because he managed to write humorous songs that weren't novelty songs, and I hadn't heard anything like that. Then I didn't hear anything until Kristofferson came along. I can remember my first contact with his stuff was an article where they had some of his lyrics. And these lyrics carried their own melody. He writes like he's got a meter built inside of him. I asked him once if he worried that much about meter (his stuff is just so perfect) and he said, 'I just throw in "oh Lord" if it doesn't balance out.'

"Jimmy Webb has written some real nice stuff. A lot of people in Nashville have excellent ears. They're Tin Pan Alley writers, but they're good at it. The Beatles wrote songs that flowed like Chuck Berry stuff and Buddy Holly stuff—which I'm sure they were very aware of when they wrote them. Their stuff caught so many different people on so many different levels—that's what was no nice about it."

What about the Dylan influence?

"Dylan's most responsible for people paying attention to lyrics. I first heard about Dylan when my brother told me the guy who wrote 'Blowin' In The Wind' sounded a lot like Jack Elliot. And I liked Jack Elliot a whole lot. I never did take Dylan's stuff word for word though. I always did like the whole balance of it, the whole feeling of it. I never did know one song all the way through, but I liked it that way and wanted to keep it that way because I thought it was a nice way to take the songs. Particularly when a lot of people went real overboard, picking the vowels apart and everything. I can't imagine what kind of pressure he went through if he let it bother him."

I asked what pains John Prine had to go through in order to rise to the ranks of the professional.

"Well, when you're an amateur and you're writing songs everybody is going to have some sort of criticism. They've never criticized a song in their life and you say 'Hey, I wrote this,' they'll say 'Well, that one part there needs changing.' So I tried to write songs that nobody could possibly criticize. But after doing that, and after recording and everything . . . I still have people come to me and tell me they loved a song for the wrong reasons. They really didn't understand it at all. I thought the songs were basically self-explanatory, but they weren't. So I just went ahead and let people like them for the wrong reasons. But I figured, I don't really have to knock myself out to explain things. I can be a little more abstract."

Prine started writing songs at the age of fourteen.

"When I started to play guitar I found that the easiest way for me to put a story down was as a song. My brother always used to hear my stuff because he taught me how to play guitar. He also taught himself how to play the fiddle, so I'd have to sit with him and play rhythm guitar. I'd sit with him for hours. If you've ever heard anybody teach himself how to play fiddle— it sounds horrible. But in return he'd listen to my songs. I'd never play them for anybody else. A lot of times I never wrote them down . . . but they were in ballad form. I'd just sing them until I got sick of them. It was easier for me to write a song than to learn somebody else's.

"In school the only thing I used to be able to do at all was when they gave me a free hand at writing dialogue. Writing nothing but dialogue. Everybody else, all these kids who were straight A students, would just bang their heads against the wall, and I'd just go, whoosh, and hand it in. The teacher would say 'Who'd you buy this from?' because I was a horrible student otherwise.

"I wrote a couple of songs in the army, but still mostly humorous stuff. It was after I got out of the army that I started writing anything serious. Of all the people I admired I never found anybody that I thought was saying exactly what I wanted to say, and that's why I wrote. But my first reaction was that I thought there must be something wrong with my songs, because they were a lot different from the stuff I'd heard. I thought if they're that much different, then why hasn't someone done them before. I'd sing them at first for friends, and they were encouraging, but I always felt like I was imposing on them. I never thought of selling songs until about a year before I went on the stage."

We discussed the various characters who have appeared in songs by John Prine.

"The names mean a lot. You know, like Loretta in 'Hello In There.' I wanted to pick a name that could be an old person's name, but I didn't want it to stick out so much. People go through phases one year where a lot of them will name their kids the same . . . and I was just thinking that it was very possible that the kind of person I had in mind could be called Loretta. And it's not so strange that it puts her in a complete time period.

"Any of the names I've ever put in a song I've spent a lot of time on. In 'Donald and Lydia' I was looking through a baby book, starting with Andrew down through Zeke. I was hollering them out like a mother calling her kids in for lunch. Take Rudy, from 'Hello In There.' We used to live in this three-room flat and across the street there was this dog who would never come in and the dog's name was Rudy. And the lady used to come out at five o'clock every night and go 'Ru-dee! Ru-dee!' And I was sitting there writing and suddenly I go 'Rudy! Yeah! I got that.'"

Finally we touched on how the singer/songwriting lifestyle, the public aspect, affected his writing.

"I would stop performing if I thought that it was really hurting my writing. I try and stay away from doing a whole lot of touring.

"Another thing—this is a result of being a recording artist. Around the time a record is finished I refuse to write for like a couple of months, even if I feel like it. Mainly because a lot of people haven't heard the new stuff, and I'll be going around doing it . . . and it's impossible for me to have a song finished and not go out and perform it. It's impossible for me to keep it locked up for six months or more."

PART SIX

Retreat and
Cease Fire:
1969–1974

(Returning
P.O.W.s)

"Ohio," by Neil Young, 1970

At Woodstock in the summer of 1969 a generation was caught in freeze frame, all together for the last time in a moment that wouldn't last beyond that moment. It was a weekend in which people were born and people died; there was community, dope, peace, and love—the music played on under the rainy skies. While Melanie sang the crowd lit candles and the sixties veterans united under the light to pray one more time to their great god rock 'n' roll.

But although the rain finally stopped, this retreat was doomed in the flood of time and tides. A short while later the death knell began sounding for the Love Generation— Altamont, presided over by the Hell's Angels, starring Mick Jagger and the Rolling Stones; Kent and Jackson State, where the enemy revealed that they had the guns *and* the numbers.

Neil Young's "Ohio," written immediately in response to the Kent State affair, released and on the radio seemingly in a matter of days, was reminiscent in its urgency of the movement heyday, when the entire population of Greenwich Village would crowd into the Village Gate to hear Phil Ochs blast the government, the liberals, the U.S. Marines, and the War. A spark of optimism flashed across the radio dial, but was left to sputter by succeeding songwriters as events conspired to sweep the sixties actions and philosophies under the rug of memory. The remaining activists were clubbed down and removed in time and consciousness as well as in music to the innocuous land of the late fifties.

"We've Only Just Begun," by Roger Nichols and Paul Williams, 1970

The super-groups of the early seventies were the Carpenters, the Partridge Family, the Osmonds, the Defrancos—who promoted a clean family apple-pie image, and, in their music and lyrical message, evoked the innocent beginnings of pop rock. Who, in fact, joined hands with slick unfelt sentiments of earlier decades and offered us a vision of modern love, holding hands down life's sweet aisle, contestants on "The Newlywed Game"—a vision the Beach Boys had long since deserted.

Of course this image had always been with us, even through the turbulent times of the sixties. We suffered glady our Monkies and Archies and Bubble Puppys with their steady diet of "Yummy Yummy," "Gimme Gimme," and "Gooey Gooey," because there was always the FM alternative. But by the seventies all of the heroes had gone down, dropped off before our eyes one by one—Lenny Bruce, Janis Joplin, Jim Morrison, Jimi Hendrix, Tim Leary, the Mahareeshi, the Kennedys, Martin Luther King—each proving to be either bogus, misguided, or fatally vulnerable to the excesses of a chaotic time.

So while John Denver smiled his way into American hearts, Bob Dylan went on an extended vacation "Watching the River Flow." Mick Jagger joined the glitter set. Phil Ochs went back to journalism. The Beatles broke up—Paul moving into film-scoring, George Harrison ascending spiritually, John Lennon cutting his hair and recording fifties oldies, and Ringo beating John to the money with his rendition of "You're Sixteen," a Sherman brothers classic of 1960, which became a huge national hit all over again in 1973–74. (The Sherman brothers, by the way, highlight, along with Bette Midler and the Pointer Sisters and Harry Nilsson, another trend with their recent Broadway lyrics and score for *Over Here,* a re-creation of the forties, starring the Andrew Sisters, minus one.)

So the nostalgia craze was a natural refuge for the disillusioned corps of sixties freaks. Entire radio bands that once played up-to-the-minute bulletins on the revolution, stayed fixed on the Flamingos, the Crests, the Monotones, and the government kept pace by attempting to move the country back to the glorious year of 1959—when the silent generation was in control (soon to grow into the silent majority)—as if to start the sixties over again, only this time to do them right.

The revival groups themselves saw the chance here for a

quick buck, so they scoured their attics for their old rock 'n' roll shoes, put together fragments of their original groups—disrupting promising careers in real estate, life insurance, and the post office—to reemerge on the circuit, singing their old songs and basking in encores that were no less sweet for having come ten to fifteen years late.

This nostalgia caused the dreamer to recall blind dates once again, acne, braces, air-raid drills, doctors, dentists, all the thrills of growing up; an experience supposedly made different by the sixties. Not so. Impressionable sub-teens hear Donny Osmond singing them old Johnny Mathis ballads and take it as a sign that the world is right again. Normalcy has returned to counter what babes had been force-fed during the passionate sixties.

The two together, nostalgia plus the gloppy "Everything Is Beautiful" sentiments of the seventies, created a whitewashed emotional tone which belied the seething, frustrated nature of the seventies. There was real music being played somewhere along the American highway, but you really had to strain yourself to hear it amidst the din of canned laughter.

"Go All The Way," by Eric Carmen, 1972

The younger generation did, however, come into a lot of sex in a hurry. The unwritten age of consent went from around eighteen down to fourteen or so (younger in urban ghettos). Your first date came clad in a see-through blouse and had been on the pill since puberty (achieved a few weeks earlier). The Raspberries (everybody's "next Beatles") hit the top of the charts in 1972 employing this vintage locker-room expression, but with a novel twist. In this lyric it's the girl asking the boy to go the route. Revolution!

It is quite possible that the song became the huge hit it did because it appealed to precisely those horny bachelors who grew up under the shadow of the bra and who were now deejays and radio programmers themselves (and on off days cased the local playgrounds for liberated fifteen-year-old chicks). Sixteen year olds were too busy screwing to buy the record. Seventeen year olds were already jaded.

These new mores enabled the youth to grow up much faster, to grow into the myriad problems of sex so much sooner, to become disenchanted at a younger age than ever! By having sex at fourteen, living together at sixteen, running the gamut of emotional highs and lows on the sex/love circuit, one might ward off marriage entirely by eighteen and turn gay at twenty. Which is approximately what happened. How could the innocent scions of the Love Generation know how dear the price of liberation would be?

The rise in homosexual chic started as camp—Bette Midler playing to a cabaret of men in bath towels; David Bowie with his flaming red mane and his depressing songs; Alice Cooper, clown prince of malicious mischief, celebrating the new generation in "Eighteen," and then going off to a beheading—his own; Iggy Pop, the Evil Knievel of rock 'n' roll, who periodically would fling himself into the raving arms of his audience. But camp or not, the image took hold. Surfeited with easy sex and looking for a new kick in the sterile seventies, the kids came up with bisexuality—boys in drag and lipstick, girls with their hair cropped close, in track team jackets, heading for the Boise junior prom.

Songs appeared with homosexual messages. "Lola," by Ray Davies is a classic, concerning the misadventures of a young man of dubious masculinity who is picked up at a bar by another person of equally dubious gender.

Songs like this, the actions of the deca/rock and glitter set, hit the original rock 'n' roll generation below the belt. They had left school, dropped acid, bucked authority, avoided the war, risked everything in Chicago . . . for this? So that their brothers and sisters should dress up in each other's clothes? There were limits, after all, to decency.

So the purists resented glitter, but the trend indicated at least the life still left in Mother Rock. As an example of one generation defiling the myths, spitting on the idols and mocking the musical past and heritage of another, you'd have to go back to the fifties and the furor created by parents over their kids adoption of Elvis Presley as spiritual and fashion model to equal it.

Deca/rock is the new degeneracy asserting itself, and degeneracy has always been one of the prime delights in the young's attraction to rock music. Not only that, deca/rock nails up the coffin of the sixties and acid rock and ships it down the river by taking all of those blissful precepts literally. Love everyone? Why not the same sex. Long hair? Style it. Colorful clothes? Trade clothes with a friend. We're all one? Bisexuality!

In 1973 the dark side is commercial. Lou Reed had a Top Twenty national hit with "Walk On The Wild Side," about a transvestite streetwalker on downs, a virtual compendium of contemporary decay. One of deca/rock's most outstanding coups was when old Mick Jagger joined the ranks for his 1973 U.S. tour, prancing around the stage in spangles and make-up, now a man, now a woman . . . now *what?* As we look to the future, Jagger stands tall (and feline) as the reigning king and queen of Decadence.

"That's The Way I've Always Heard It Should Be," by Jacob Brackman and Carly Simon, 1971

"Younger Generation," by John Sebastian, 1968

The eternal changing of the guard. Young kids think their folks are square no matter if their folks are stoned potheads. Nothing so passé as last year's craze.

Survivors of the sixties reluctantly realized that the dream was truly over, an era passed them by. Having been promised eternal youth by the polo shirt-clad rock stars, they took adulthood hard. All during the sixties there was hope that adolescence might be stretched past thirty, so people avoided making commitments. But in the seventies the pendulum swung back on them, knocking all those sweet thoughts awry.

Perhaps it was time to awaken, trudge on back to school, get married, trim the beard, look for work, cut down on the smoking, start reading the papers again? Just as Scott Fitzgerald and his twenties flappers had their Depression, the sixties heads and hippies got depressed in the seventies when faced with these options, thus giving rise to your acidhead accountants who trip on weekends, dope-smoking lushes who need that joint before dinner to unwind, long-haired rock-freak schoolteachers in dungarees who are indistinguishable from the students they teach, earthmother love-goddess communal housewife and liberated stud husband sex tag-team remembering how it used to be. When sixties nostalgia invades the radio (around 1978 or so) it may well be too painful to listen to, evoking memories of possibilities that seemed so near. Then again, it may seem then to be less than it was, hopelessly naive and false. Many in the generation, approaching or just past thirty, have already begun turning their backs on the past, giving up drugs altogether, what's more, repudiating them as adolescent playthings. By the time marijuana gets legalized most adults may have all but given it up.

So, in song anyway, Carly Simon gets married, half against her will—Hear that, James?—and John Sebastian has a heart to heart with his son. Funny though, John, in his lyrics, thought his kid would be further out than *he* was, chomping LSD for breakfast, XYZ for lunch; but it may be that the kids brought up by rock 'n' roll parents will rebel in a different way—much like children of drunks will become teetotalers. Already on campus we see short hair coming back, beer returning to favor, a new career and work ethic filling the libraries and study halls. No riots this year. Streaking (the new campus thrill) seems more related to the fifties craze of mooning than to the sixties shocking public nudity at rock festivals. Even exhibitionism in the seventies is regressive. The bra is making a hurried comeback. Where will it end?

"Superfly," by Curtis Mayfield, 1972

In the seventies the most sensual and intense music around is rhythm and blues (just as in the early fifties). This music is vital and real because it still emanates from and mirrors the city-experience, while white rock 'n' roll has left that terrain by and large for the suburbs (except for certain hard-rock groups like the New York Dolls). But the experience to be found in cities everywhere these days is not pretty. It is a landscape of slums, populated by those too poor or atrophied to move out.

The Lower East Side and Haight-Ashbury, once meccas for tourists and the pseudo-poor, have been left to the rats; the head shops abandoned and transformed into laundromats. The Fillmores East and West have closed. Mainly it is blacks and Third World minorities that inhabit the city. The whites have fled to greener pastures. Even New York City has lost some of the glamour it had in the old days when the Drifters wanted to make it "On Broadway."

Now there is paranoia, junkies ripping each other off for the next fix. The O'Jays named the disease in their 1972 hit "Backstabbers." The Temptations tell of a "Runaway Child," riding high on "Cloud Nine." Marvin Gaye asks us to ponder "What's Goin' On?" Meanwhile Curtis Mayfield and Isaac Hayes unravel the drug myth 1970s-style in "Superfly" and "Shaft," respectively.

Philadelphia is once again prominent as a music scene, the home of Gamble and Huff, a more mellow expression of the dire times, the Chi-lites, the Spinners, the Intruders, Al Green, a lulling sound to offset the rigors of reality. Blacks have lived with hard times before—forever—their music shows just this survival quality.

Nineteen seventy-four finds heroin and cocaine as the twin

addictions of the year; the opiums of high and low culture respectively—the upper class burning themselves out in a frenzy of self-love, the lower class harmonizing in a stupor of self-hate.

"Both Sides Now," by Joni Mitchell, 1968

Rock 'n' roll has gone from innocence to knowledge to innocence to knowledge . . . and now hangs suspended looking for redemption, having fooled with the apple once too often. The new breed watched the old breed fall; they won't make the same mistakes again. The spate of crises the nation is going through in 1974, revealing all the prophesies of the sixties to be true, does not provide this redemption, cannot ease the pain of being the generation on the downslide, watching its successors hail the sunshine and close their eyes to the rain.

If, as they say, bad times produce happy epics (who says?) then the seventies are grim indeed. For it is well known that "Rainy Days and Mondays" always bring the Carpenters down; that "Sunshine On My Shoulder" makes John Denver "high"; and that a Rod McKuen song, "Seasons In The Sun," about dying, currently resides near the top of the charts. Does anyone see the rainclouds? FM radio is no longer a trusted weathervane. And Bob Dylan claims that love is the answer, but no one really believes he means that and that only.

Redemption is found neither in the signs of an imminent sixties revival, starring the Highwaymen and The Kingston Trio with their banjo picks and stripe-ed collars . . . or in the rumored reformation of certain treasured lost groups like Crosby, Stills, Nash and Young; the Electric Flag; the Blues Project; or even the Beatles. That kind of thing may well be better off living in the past.

Many among the generation have already mourned the loss: Don Mclean bidding farewell to Miss "American Pie"; Harry Chapin tooling around in his "Taxi," never having learned to fly; Paul Simon bemoaning our shattered dreams in "American Tune"; Joni Mitchell in "Blue," castigating a sixties advocate

of "acid, guns and grass, needles, booze and ass. . . ." Jackson
Browne still searching for "Everyman" and Neil Young wondering why "You can't be twenty on Sugar Mountain."

However, in all this, there is cause for a final note of optimism now that the Cult of Youth is over. The groupies have
all left the party; nobody is looking at the generation anymore;
things can return to the way they were in the twilight of the
dawning of Aquarius. Soon drugs may be legal. You can show
everything in a movie, write whatever you please on your fore-
head for all I care. The true artists of the age will be left to
create in peace, safe in the underground where they will be free
from corruption. Their fantasies will not be consumed by the
public for years to come. End of note of optimism.

But what of rock? In 1974 have we reached the limits of
growth? Or will the music keep moving onward and upward
with its parent generation, proving to be as valid for the later
years as it was for the early ones, while still having parts of
it dangling down into the camps of the upcoming children? I
mean, will there be writers to sing about the joys of being
thirty, or will we be doomed to hearing adolescents chanting
sagas of puppy love until we're in our graves? Will the rock
writers produce, as the Broadway writers did, well into their
geriatric years? Will there indeed be a Woodstock in St. Peters-
burg at Al Lang Field with a seventy-year-old Bob Dylan (and
a white-haired Robbie Robertson on lead guitar) singing "Like
A Rolling Gall-Stone" to our undiminished adulation (and
hacking coughs)?

Or will we have to find out about the rest of our lives in
books the way the other generations did (or didn't)? Or will
we fall into identifying our images with those portrayed on the
silver screen? Or worse, on television?

MELANIE SAFKA

Melanie emerged on the music scene, a tiny figure in the rain at Woodstock in 1969, alone onstage with her guitar and her songs. She has since gone on to become one of the most popular of our female singer/songwriters of the seventies.

At the start her songs were often childlike odes to simplicity, taking up the stance of the outsider, the loser in the social caste system of growing up. Eventually they became deeper and more personal, her delivery becoming more intense.

Like Joni Mitchell, one can see Melanie's voice and lyrical content growing and maturing with the years. Her undiminished legion of fans have seen her through marriage and a baby. And they come by the thousands to the concert halls whenever she performs.

The interview with Melanie took place at her apartment overlooking Central Park in New York City. Her six-month-old daughter, Leilah, provided a musical score for our conversation.

"I've been writing ever since I can remember—poems, essays, songs; sometimes it's only a sentence or a word. I'm terribly undisciplined about it. I can't sit down and just say I'm going to write today. I have to wait until I'm in the mood for it. I'm not a very neat songwriter. I don't always write down my ideas. I always figure if it's meant to be a song I'll remember it, if it's not I won't. What happens to me all the time is that I'll remember a song I was *going* to write that I thought was so good, but I can't remember what it was. Sometimes I'll have a whole lot of ideas, but I won't remember any of them.

"I'll be taking a walk, because that happens a lot while I'm walking, especially in the morning . . . I'll get all kinds of ideas,

energy just pours in and I get all these ideas and then by the time I get back to the house or something, they're just gone. They're not there anymore. But I don't get too upset about it.

"For me, getting ideas is the best part of living. It's the best part of writing songs. Once you get the idea it's sort of boring to follow it through, because you know what you mean—why do you have to sit there and explain it to everybody? And you have to explain it in three verses, and you may need six hours to explain this idea, or else just shut up about it altogether 'cause it's not going to make sense in three verses. So that's why I guess a lot of my songs don't make sense to some people. It's too hard to explain some things, and it's incredibly simple to just say the sentence and let the person get the essence of it. Explaining every detail is boring. I hate detailed explanations."

I asked her if the city is a source of her energy.

"It depends on how I'm relating to the city at the time. When you feel good in a big city you really feel good. When you feel bad it's hard to get the energy, because it's just an attack on you. When I'm attacked I can't do anything. I just fold up. When I'm at such a low point I can't write, but when I remember, maybe I will. Misery is no fun, but you might get something out of it after you've experienced it.

"Sometimes something gets to me so bad that I do write it and it makes me feel better, but I can't do that deliberately.

"Right now I'm not in a very productive mood. But I'm getting a lot of good feelings about things. I'm more balanced than I ever was, and that balance, when it gets thrown off, is when I write. When I'm centered I don't have to say anything, because I *am* and that's all; it doesn't matter what I say."

I wondered if most of her writing came out of depression. If so, why didn't she write about feeling good?

"It's a hard thing to handle, feeling good, because it's a very of-the-moment thing. People don't know how to live in the moment. They're just living in the memory of something or in the anxiety of something or the anticipation of something.

So right away, as soon as you're feeling good, you're saying 'Oh my God, it's not going to last.' You can't stop to write about it.

"I think I write sometimes when I'm really elated, but then again, it's off-balance in the other direction. Where I'm at right now is the balance that I see a rabbit in, or a fish. It's not the balance, for instance, of a lion. It doesn't inspire me to put anything down, but it's a good learning time."

I asked if she writes about things that have actually happened to her.

"No, that's not usually how it happens. I've wanted to write that way because I've been at some incredible events and I've wanted to put them into song, but I don't really know how to do it. Sometimes just one little idea will come out of a situation, but it may only start the song.

"I always wonder if there are too many I's in my songs. I wish there could be less. 'Maybe Not For A Lifetime' and 'Love To Lose Again' seem to have less I and Me . . . but I'm not prone to writing objective songs. I can't fool myself in a song. I usually know why I'm writing it. The training I've had in my life taught me to be honest with myself, to know what I was really feeling.

"These days perhaps I've been dwelling on the theme of being alone. I know that all of us are alone and that thought comes through in a lot of my lyrics. To understand being alone was an important step for me. I always felt if you were with somebody you didn't have to account for yourself totally. But when you know you're alone you know that you're responsible for everything that you do. Nobody can share it with you. That's the way it is."

I wanted to know about her early experience with music, especially rock 'n' roll.

"I didn't like rock 'n' roll. I didn't like Elvis or the Beatles or anybody. Later on I liked the Beatles. I didn't get into Bob Dylan until the *Nashville Skyline* album. All through high school I was really a folk-music purist. Joan Baez and Judy Collins weren't folk singers to me. I was more influenced by Peggy Seeger, Susan Reed recordings that were made in the Ozarks by funny-voiced ladies . . . Jean Ritchie.

"I don't remember radio at that time at all. My uncle used to play me folk-music records and also very source-type classical music. Before that, my mother had a lot of blues and jazz records that I liked to hear and she was also a jazz singer and she sang to me. But when I was thirteen I sort of rebelled against my mother's music and got into folk.

"I'm not sure how strong an influence folk music was on me, but my feelings about it changed when I started to express myself in my own music. In fact some of the songs that I used to get very passionate about are really silly to me now. Wordy things, love songs . . . but they still stand because they're true, although when I try to translate them into today's world they're unrelated to me."

I asked if she'd had any fantasies about making it in music.

"I didn't really have a strong fantasy; it was definitely in the back of my mind, but way, way back. And when things started to unfold I said 'Oh yeah, I've always wanted that.' But as I would get to each thing it was never as much fun as I'd imagined it. It wasn't what I thought it was going to be. There are always disappointments in everything, in winning things.

"Having an album out was a great disappointment. It was just that I felt more would happen. When I recorded 'Lay Down' I just said 'Oh, I hope I just die. I don't ever want to do anything; this is just the greatest thing. I don't want to have to do anything else.' I knew I'd come down from it. I have fantasies now, but they're not as easy to define.

"When an album comes out I like to hear that it's selling, or it's number this or number that. But after the first couple albums I didn't really concern myself with that too much. As long as I knew I could continue singing and writing, I was pleased.

"As far as skillful writing goes, *Stoneground Words* was one of my best albums, but there are a lot of songs in there that I know people didn't hear."

What about singles?

"I have a great advertising sense. I know when something is commercial. I don't mean to know it, and I don't deliberately write that way, but when I do, I know it. As songs they're not any better or any worse than the rest. I don't know when a song is uncommercial, I just know when one is. Although I was a little surprised about 'Peace Will Come.' I wasn't sure about 'Lay Down.' I was sure it was the greatest thing I ever did, but I wasn't sure whether people were going to like it . . . and I didn't care.

"I don't remember ever being in the country when I've had a hit record. I don't deliberately leave, but I've rarely been around to appreciate the hits I've had."

I asked Melanie how she felt about her "image."

"After my second album on Buddah Records I felt like I was imitating myself, which was really a strange thing. I said 'This isn't what I am now, this is an imitation of me!' It wasn't done deliberately, to please an audience or a type of person or anything; it was just secure, comfortable; nobody was saying to stop. But I realized it and I changed slowly.

"In fact, my whole first album I sing very differently. The songs have grown. In performance I'll do the songs differently every time, so it's a different song now than it was when I wrote it. I have a whole new way of looking at early songs such as 'Baby Guitar' and 'Deep Down Low.'

"I think some people didn't really listen to those songs because of the image that my old record company was cultivating. They were attempting to portray me as a naive flower-child and they jumped on everything that lent itself to strengthening that image, including some of the songs I wrote, such as 'Beautiful People' and 'I Don't Eat Animals.' Songs like 'Baby Guitar' and 'Deep Down Low' got no emphasis from the record company, so they received less attention from the public. I've changed the meaning of a lot of my early songs. I'll stop singing songs I can't identify with."

We talked about the way she works.

"Usually a good part of the song will come out at once, words and music at the same time. The best ones come that way. The finishing touches I always have to work on, and sometimes I don't, so they just get put out not exactly finished. But I always finish them eventually. It'll just be a matter of putting two different words in, or humming something in the middle, or making a bridge.

"My husband, Peter, helps me a lot. Most of the time I like him to be there when I'm writing a song. He's very good at getting ideas straight. Sometimes I get mixed up.

"I really like a song that completes itself. Like, 'Maybe Not For A Lifetime,' from *Magrugada,* because it's a whole thought and I really worked it out. It was work; it wasn't just that I got lazy and sloughed it off. I really finished it and I like that. I never was disciplined in the beginning; I was just purely emotional. But I'll tell you, some of those earlier songs are better than the ones I'm writing now. Just because you've been writing a long time doesn't make your songs any better. I really believe that.

"When I finish something and I like it, I'll sing it. If I write a song two seconds before a show, I'll sing it in the show. Most of what I write I eventually record. I don't hide things. I once put a line in a song 'Here I Am'—'Nothing left, so here I am/I didn't save for later, got nothing in the can.'

"In other people's songs, I generally like passionate lyrics. I think people are sort of afraid of songs like that. They're afraid to risk anything. They like a song with a way out. I'd say people are afraid to commit themselves to anything. There's a lot of fear around."

I asked Melanie, in closing, if she ever felt guilty while writing—if she ever used it as an escape to a better world.

"I never feel guilty about writing, but I'm definitely escaping. I don't feel guilty, I feel relieved. I indulge myself completely."

TIM RICE

First Tom Sankey brought *The Golden Screw* to off-off Broadway. Then, summarizing rapidly, Al Carmines applied his lyric touch to the outrageous *Home Movies* and *Promenade* of Rosalyn Drexler at the Judson Theatre in Greenwich Village; actor-writers Rado and Ragni got cab fare uptown from Joseph Papp and put "Rock Theater" on Broadway with *Hair!* Following in the wake of that enormous breakthrough came some epic bashes, chief among them being *Godspell* by Stephen Schwartz and *Jesus Christ, Superstar* by Tim Rice and Andrew Lloyd Webber.

Superstar—the record album, the play, the movie, the original cast album, the soundtrack, "I Don't Know How To Love Him" by Yvonne Elliman, the semi-hit single of the title by Murray Head—has been a huge money-maker, as has *Godspell*—the movie, the play, and "Day by Day"—to say nothing of those out of the Rado and Ragni songbag—"Hair!" by the Cowsills; "Easy To Be Hard," by Three Dog Night; "Age Of Aquarius," by the Fifth Dimension; "Starshine," by Oliver; and "Frank Mills" (the movie version is now in production). And we are still awaiting Ken Russell's filmed spectacle of Peter Townshend's *Tommy,* which has been everything from opera to ballet to rock concerto.

On the other hand, whatever happened to Tom Sankey?

The interview with Tim Rice took place at the Plaza Hotel in New York City where Tim was staying on a brief visit to these shores.

"We had the tune first every time. Occasionally I might say 'I've got a fantastic title,' but very rarely. On the bigger projects like *Superstar* I would first provide a framework, a kind of a plot. I'd say, for example, 'This song is going to be a violent song. It's got to say a, b, and c, therefore we need a certain kind of tune.' Andrew would then write a melody knowing what sort of tune was needed and then I'd put words to it after that. In the case of *Superstar*, obviously we both discussed the framework, too.

"So he'd play a tune for me and I'd pick it up. If I couldn't pick it up quickly, obviously it wasn't a good tune. I'd tape it on a recorder if I happened to have one on me, or if not I'd just have it in my skull. Often I'll write down just nonsense words like 'I want you in the bath' or 'I need you on the floor,' anything just to remember the rhythm.

"I have written lyrics without actually knowing the tune. Once or twice in an emergency Andrew has rung up or written to me and said 'Just write lyrics to I love you my baby I need you,' and I would then write something that's completely different, but it would scan. Later he would show me how the melody goes.

"Usually I've got the tune in my head. I can play piano well enough so that if Andrew gives me the chords I can play the tune. Lyric writing for me is a nine to five office thing. You have to sit down and wade through it, like a crossword puzzle. You get a nice high, I suppose, if you write something good, but it's more like solving a puzzle. You simply get the feeling of 'Yeah, that's it!' But you have to work hard at it. I don't walk down the street and get inspired.

"The number one thing to make me like a song is a good tune. I don't care if it's corny, or if it's rock, it just has to have a bit of a melody. That's why I like people like John Fogerty, whom I think is one of the great rock writers. In addition to the excitement and whatever else he has, he writes beautiful tunes.

"I don't think I could write lyrics like Paul Simon's particularly well. He's a brilliant lyricist, but I tend to think more theatrically. I think that the kind of lyrics I write are in one sense more old-fashioned. They're more in the style of the traditional theater, and they tend to be more specific whereas Paul Simon and Dylan, of course, write more often in abstract. They use a lot of imagery, which is great, but that's not really my sort of song. I do better with the more factual stuff. I can write a fairly amusing point number. I never could have written 'Proud Mary' or 'Mr. Tamborine Man,' although I'd have loved to.

"I do follow the theater quite a lot now. I usually find if I come to New York for four or five days I'll see four or five plays. [Although in town for only two nights, Mr. Rice managed to see *Jumpers* and *Over Here.*] I always did follow the theater quite a lot for an average bloke, compared with the other people at school, and the way I follow the record industry is phenomenal. I could name you every artist on the Hot Hundred. But I don't have a fanatical interest in the theater. Andrew was the one with the burning ambition to write for the theater. I just did it because it seemed like a good idea at the time."

Rice and Andrew Lloyd Webber met in 1965. Both had been trying to break through in the pop market, Rice as a singer, Webber as a composer. On the side, Andrew was working on a show.

"He said, 'I've got backing for a musical if I can come up with a lyricist,' and I said I'd have a go. And although the musical came to nothing, we discovered that we could work well as a team. So it was as a result of Andrew that I found myself trying to be a lyricist, whereas I'd been trying to be a pop singer."

Their first effort concerned Dr. Barnardo, an East End figure of the Victorian Age.

"It was a bit like *Oliver,* except it wasn't as good. It had some good things and I think anybody listening would have said those lads are quite promising."

Later on they got their next assignment.

"We were then asked by a schoolmaster friend of ours to write anything we liked, just a fifteen or twenty minute piece, for his kids at school for the end-of-the-term concert. It was a great comedown, because we'd had all those visions of a fantastic show on Broadway and in the West End of London, and now we were writing something for eight- to ten-year-old kids. There was no money in it, but we thought we'd do it. The schoolmaster said that if it went well he might get a publishing company interested and perhaps it would become something that schools would use.

"So we did it on spec, for nothing. It was called *Joseph and the Amazing Technicolor Dreamcoat*. We chose a Bible story purposely because we wanted something that would appeal to teachers, so that they might buy it for their kids. And we made it funny because we wanted the kids to be amused. So it was a big success at this concert and the publishers who'd been asked along by the school said they loved it and would like to publish it. So we made it into a half hour piece, expanded from the original twenty minutes and they printed it up in a book and we made fifty pounds each and it did very well.

"For a couple of years before *Superstar* we were earning a small amount of money from *Joseph*, and of course, since *Superstar*, *Joseph* has boomed. We expanded it to ninety minutes and it has now been quite a big hit in England as a professional show."

About six months after finishing *Joseph*, the songwriting team of Webber and Rice felt it was time to begin work on something new.

"For a long time I'd had a great interest in Judas Iscariot, whom I thought was a fascinating character. Even before I met Andrew I thought it would be great to write a play about Judas in which Jesus is only a minor character. Or tell the story with

Jesus as a major character, but tell it from Judas' point of view. If you study the Bible, which I have as a result of writing *Superstar,* you'll find that the character of Judas Iscariot is nonexistent. He doesn't really have any motives. He doesn't say anything, and he's only mentioned a couple of times. The Gospels were written sometime later, and it was convenient and easy to make Judas 100 percent bad, a figure of evil, the exact opposite of Christ. It was obviously helpful to the story, also, to have it blamed on one guy. But I couldn't believe that this was plausible. These are not colossally original thoughts, but I still had this idea about trying to do a thing from Judas' point of view.

"After the success of *Joseph* one realized that one could mix modern music and the Bible. So we thought, let's have a go at writing a play on Judas.

"Well, it was obviously a heavy undertaking and we still at that point had had no commercial success. One little thing in schools wasn't going to make people fork out 50,000 pounds to produce a show. So we decided to do it via record. We were producing a few of our own songs at that point and I had worked at EMI, so we had some connections in the record world. So it was for economic reasons that we were forced to try to get somebody to back a record, when we really wanted to write a show.

"After being turned down by several people, we got MCA records in London interested, but they said it would be too expensive to do the whole LP. They said they'd put out a single, 'And if that goes, it will justify spending all that money for an album. It will prove there's a market for it.'

"This was late summer of 1969. We just had an outline, the framework, which was a lot of work, but there were only a few tunes and a few ideas. We hadn't thought in terms of a single, but we thought the actual song 'Superstar,' would be possible. So we went away and polished it up and took it back to them.

"As soon as the single was finished, even though we didn't know whether it was going to be a hit or not, we went away and began writing the rest of the album, because we felt that we wanted to do it regardless. This was around Christmas 1969. In about three or four months we'd done 80 percent of it. Meanwhile the single, by Murray Head, began taking off. It was a small hit in the U.S. and a big hit in Brazil and Belgium and Australia.

"On English sales alone, the project would have been killed, but the worldwide sales were big enough for MCA to say go ahead. By about February of 1970 . . . we'd written most of the work . . . and we then had the colossal job of actually getting people to sing on the album. That almost took longer than writing it. It was like a military operation.

"In October it was released in England and America and it sunk in England. It was an immediate total flop. No one wanted to know about it. It got very good reviews, but it didn't get any airplay. But we'd been booked to come to the states, because MCA liked what it had been given. So we thought at least we'll get one trip out of it. But when we got here, at the airport we were met by a great army of people, press and everything, and we suddenly realized it was going to be a big hit here.

"Ironically, the whole thing really was not what we'd aimed for, because we were still really trying to write for the theater, and this album was a kind of demonstration record."

I asked Tim what he'd been doing since *Superstar*.

"Our output has declined colossally, largely because we've been so busy running around the world doing an awful lot of work connected with it, but not actually creative work. Of course, since *Superstar* we've expanded *Joseph* to twice as long as it was. An awful lot of pop songs we'd written, the tunes have gone into the new bits of *Joseph* with new lyrics. Andrew has done a film score and I'm doing some broadcasting. I have a show every week on English radio as a disc jockey, playing oldies. So we've been quite busy, but we definitely got a bit off the rails in terms of output.

"Which I don't think matters. First, it takes a long time to get over the shell shock of something like *Superstar,* and second we don't really want to hurry into something else. Take Lionel Bart who wrote *Oliver;* he's a great writer, he's written an awful lot of pop hits in England, but he did come out with a lot of stuff very quickly after *Oliver,* and each one didn't do quite so well as the one before. I don't know how he worked, but I often think if he'd waited three or four years and put all his best things into one, it might have worked out better. So we can afford to wait, but I do think that about now is the time to do something else."

I asked about his leisure time pursuits.

"I play records; I collect records, file them, look them up on the charts. I watch a lot of cricket, play cricket, play football, watch soccer, read history, take the dogs out for a walk, play piano badly. Not writing doesn't particularly bother me. I never have and never will have any message for anybody. No message for the world at all."

He did have one message to America, however, that I promised I'd pass along.

"Oh yes, I'd love Elvis to do one of my songs."

HARRY CHAPIN

Harry Chapin is probably the most novelistic of our songwriters. Using techniques most often found in prose, he has created a series of story songs, all highly plotted and deftly characterized.

He is also one of the more verbal and articulate writers whom I talked to, able to expound at length on any number of song-

writing aspects. He had, in fact, one week before our talk, delivered a major address to the American Guild of Authors and Composers on the subject, in addition to having been interviewed on the art and craft of songwriting on numerous occasions.

Just prior to my interview, Harry was questioned by radio station WPLJ in New York concerning his professional endeavors. Nevertheless, when my appointed time came around, I plunged in with a set of my own queries, which Harry answered with a speed and precision equalled only—in my experience—by Phil Ochs. At a local diner, over a shrimp salad sandwich, his three-year-old daughter spilling orange juice to the left of him, Harry Chapin held forth on his favorite topic until closing time.

To properly appreciate this 33⅓ interview, the reader should turn his record player to 45 RPM.

"I think when you're in a mass artform like music, by definition you're asking people to listen. An audience can be approached two different ways, as a mob or as a collection of individuals with a potential for positive action. I would like to think I'm approaching them that second way, rather than the first. I would like to think my songs can appeal to teenyboppers and hippies and hardhats and grandmothers and young marrieds . . . that they talk about basic things ["W.O.L.D."— "forty-five going on fifteen"—"Taxi," about people who have broken dreams back in high school] not based on fads or on momentary ups and downs of what's 'in' or 'out.' I'm not trying to write for a teenybop audience; I'm trying to write to a human audience, which hopefully applies to teenyboppers too.

"I've got a constant internal battle in terms of the way I write. Paul Leka, my producer, said an interesting thing. He said, 'Some people write for themselves and some people write for other people; each deserves the audience he asks for.' I mean, if you're really writing to be in a garrett and sing for yourself, then you're not trying to communicate and you should not be hurt that you're not getting heard.

"But I don't think it's necessarily an exclusive thing. I'm trying to do both. I'm writing for myself and for people, and I think if you've got an accurate antenna and you pick out the place where you have something to say and tie that in with other people, hopefully you're not going to propagandize but sensitize. I don't think the whole idea of giving other people answers is the answer, because the minute you have an answer, that's a static reality and life is not static, life is a flux. The minute you put yourself in one stance you're going to find within a very short time that it no longer applies, because life will change right out from under you. When you propagandize you say you have in fact an answer. When you sensitize you're creating attitudes, something that will apply to a lot of different people, that will give them, not an answer, but a question that might be interesting for them to ask themselves.

"The standard explanation I give as to why my story songs are different than most songs is that most songs are what I call attitudinal songs. The songwriter has an attitude. 'I Wanna Hold Your Hand,' 'Fire and Rain,' 'You've Got A Friend.' And the writer's sensitivity exposes that attitude to the audience. In other words, he is the receiving organism, and he describes what he has received. What I try to do is create the situation that created the attitude. Hopefully what I do is physically create the atmosphere and let the listener feel it, rather than tell him how it affected me.

"So, like in 'Taxi,' there's not a single line that tells how the guy or the girl felt. It's a very cinematic technique. But it's also a very uneconomical technique. That's why my songs are so long. I literally put you in that cab and let you experience. It's a more involving form of music than sitting and hearing somebody sing 'I'm lonely.'

"I find I'm more successful in the live form, when I'm there in person performing, because, frankly, it's a somewhat egotistical stance on my part to think that somebody is going to sit for ten minutes and listen to a song. When I'm there in person I have a large part to do with successful communication. At a concert you're setting the visual context, the aural context as well as the oral. When you're on record that person listening may be ironing, making love; they may be trying to ignore the song. You're in a much less controllable situation. And since my songs ask a lot of the listener, it's a little easier for me to communicate in person. The only communication you get from an album is the sales report three months later, or numbers of the charts.

"My songs are not as broad a musical form, say, as a Lennon and McCartney song or a Dylan song. Some of their songs are indestructable, in the sense that anybody could sing them. They can be put in almost any context. I'm afraid that my songs aren't that way; they're too individualized. I mean, although hopefully they can affect everybody, Andy Williams is just not going to sing 'Sniper,' although I'd love to hear it."

Earlier in the afternoon, I sat in on the interview at WPLJ. Harry mentioned the influence of his wife on his work, and I asked him to elaborate on this.

"Well, basically a person needs accurate input from people who are not at all impressed by any stature or notoriety. The ultimate extent would be somebody like Bob Dylan. Nobody really has the stature and credibility, I would think, to talk to Bob Dylan honestly about his songs. Well I'm lucky enough that my wife, who's really a better writer than I am, is very willing to give me accurate feedback about what I do, which is an incredibly valuable resource. She's very good at cutting down things and saying 'What are you talking about here?' I've gotten off course a bunch of times, the star trip and everything else. You can't help it to a certain extent. But to the extent that I'm fairly stable right now, it has a lot to do with her.

"Also, she comes up with good ideas. I mean, that song I

just sang in the studio, 'What Made America Famous,' basically comes out of a thing where she was saying 'You should write a song about a volunteer fire department and name it "Answering the Call." ' Now, I took it to a whole other place, but I'm a believer in recognizing good ideas. My wife happens to be a fantastic poet and I've been very lucky to have her with me.

"I argue with her, but in the arguing I find out where I really am. If I can't argue well, I say 'Hey man, you're kidding yourself.' For instance, I thought about the 'Answering the Call' idea, but it wasn't right for me. I couldn't find the hook—the way to do it. The way the song turned out, it's actually like looking at a prism that's gradually spinning and you're seeing different facets of it as you go around, going from sarcastic despair to hope on the other side.

"The key to a song for me is a general idea of what the song is about. The magic moment is when you find the hook. In most people's songs the hook is a line, but in my songs the hook would be the way to bring the concept alive. In 'Sniper,' the hook for that song is when I suddenly realized that it was a conversation between the sniper and the people who were shooting back at him. It wasn't just an exchange of bullets. At that point the whole song followed. In 'Taxi,' when I had the lines 'She was gonna be an actress and I was gonna learn to fly,' when I had that, then the song grew both ways from there.

"Since I'm not working strictly in a chorus–verse form, the key to my songs is a little bit different than anybody else's. My songs are very linear. There are two tricks that you need. You've got to be aurally and lyrically geared to the fact that since you don't always have a chorus reoccurring, you've got the extra problem of re-seducing people all the way through, to keep their interest up. And then also you've got to write enough good lines and enough good images so that if somebody tunes in the song halfway through, they're gonna be wondering what the first half was like. Some stories tend to be all or nothing, if you don't start at the first line you're in trouble.

"Each of my songs has had technical problems to solve. 'Better Place To Be' is a story within a story, where a guy is in a barroom with a waitress, then they have a flashback, with him telling a whole story, and then they cut back again. So there was a problem in terms of both melody and lyric, to make sure people know where they are.

"Here's the influence of my wife again. The first song on my first album is called 'Put Your Light On Please.' Well, one night she was working on a poem and about a half hour after we went to bed, she got a great idea so she said 'Harry, could you put your light on please?' So I said 'Hey, that's a great idea for a song.' While she was writing down her idea, I wrote down a song from her line!".

In the fall of 1974 Harry Chapin's name could be atop a Broadway marquee, for a musical entitled *The Great Divide*.

"It's about a young man, age sixteen in 1960, growing up to 1974 and assessing where he is, his own life, and all the movements he's gotten into—all the zingers that have been thrown his way. He's a young, idealistic guy who's probably been re-shaped by too many moods and shifts and everything else.

"It's called *The Great Divide* and it's him at the great divide of age thirty, dividing the future and the past, adulthood and childhood. I wrote the book and the songs. Six or seven of the songs are on my records, the rest are new. In all there's thirty songs and seven poems.

"One of the interesting things about this, the exhilarating thing, is that I've been working over about an eight-year period with some vague form of this and gotten turned down every time. This one final version at this point seems like it's gotten somewhere. And I know I haven't pandered. I've written as good a thing as I can. The nice thing is when you're aiming at that and finding that yes, it does affect other people too."

I asked Harry for his assessment of the arts in 1974.

"I would have to say the two most viable artforms right now are music, because of the whole recording medium, and film, which is the only uniquely twentieth-century artform. And they're both still being explored. Music is tremendously exciting now because you've got a tremendous cross-cultural flow. Indian ragas and African rhythms and realistic lyrics and English ballad form and American blues. Just as they find with breeding, when you get different kinds of strains together you get stronger individuals, in music right now it's so strong and vital because it's got all these influxes.

"Another thing that I find interesting is the change since 1967. There has never been a time that I know of in human history when the music form and the basic social tenor of the time was so one to one as it was then. It was like the music *was* the lifestyle at that moment.

"But right now you have fragmentation. Grand Funk Railroad, the Jackson Five, the Osmond Brothers, all have their own audience. There's a Harry Chapin audience, a Seals and Crofts audience, even Dylan now has only a specialized audience. In one sense it's good because it means there's a whole bunch of different possibilities, but at the same time it doesn't have the basic thrust, for example, as 1964 had. In 1964 the Beatles and folk/rock provided a general thrust.

"In music right now you've got stock taking and specialization, everybody trying to take their own form up a few notches. It puts interesting pressures on the business, because the record execs are much more comfortable with general trends, because they know how to follow them. If you've got a Beatles, then all of a sudden you can have a Dave Clark Five and a Rolling Stones. The problem that comes out of having all these different audiences is that the execs have to take each thing in terms of its own validity, which they're not really equipped to handle."

In summarizing his attitude about songwriting, Harry Chapin spoke a volume in less than thirty seconds.

"A description I often use about what I'm trying to do in writing is something said by Eddie Sachs, the racing driver who got killed at Indianapolis. He said 'I know I'm driving perfectly when I take a turn at 163.1 miles per hour, and I know if I went at 163.2 I'd be out of control.' That's when he knew he was driving perfectly. What I would like to do is be on that edge, pushing the boundaries out to what is possible in the song form to reach a lot of people, and at the same time reach a lot of people.

"There's an awful lot of writers who drive around that track at ninety miles per hour, waving. . . .

"In my mind at this point I'm a professional. A professional is one who is doing something that he cares about and has worked at hard enough so that he's good at it. I'm in the lucky position of caring deeply about what I do and at the same time doing it for a living. If you make money at your dream, you can't do better."

LINDA CREED

In the seventies the most popular form of music is, once again, R&B, also known as Soul. Emanating primarily from Philadelphia, it is a laid-back vision, emphasizing lush harmony. A softer trip than the Motown sound of the sixties, it is no less real. In 1971 or 1972 you could inspect the Top Ten on any given week and find at least five tunes credited to black artists and/or writers. And what Smokey Robinson and Eddie Holland were to the literature of Motown, Kenny Gamble and Leon Huff are to this new sound, "Philly-Soul."

Spinning out melodies and arrangements for such stalwart groups as the Spinners, the Chi-lites, the O'Jays, the Delfonics, is the master composer of the Gamble–Huff Organization, Tommy Bell. In fact, today the company is known as Gamble–Huff–Bell. And working right alongside Tommy, perhaps the reigning poetess of the Top Ten, is Linda Creed. It's just a

matter of time, I suspect, before the company will have to change its name again, adding on another partner.

My interview with Linda Creed took place at the offices of Gamble–Huff–Bell (and Creed) in downtown Philadelphia.

"I started writing songs in 1969. Originally I was a singer and Tommy Bell tried to help me, but I was unsuccessful. When I came back to Philadelphia Tommy suggested I get a job as a secretary at Gamble–Huff. I figured, as long as I'm around music, I don't care. Then one day he said 'Hey Creed, have you ever tried writing lyrics?' I told him I'd written poems, but never thought of them as lyrics. So we tried it. We sat down and wrote 'Free Girl,' and that was it—ever since then we've been writing together.

"Tommy and I have always worked in a very structured way. We'll sit down at the piano together and write a tune for a particular artist. There's no excess. I would never go home, say, and knock out forty lyrics and bring them in. It's always been very structured and it still is. Originally, we'd sit down together and Tommy would play a melody and I'd write a line at a time or wherever I could fit it in, and then I'd go back and polish it up. As we both became more professional and as I began to get a method to my madness, I would just get a tape of the melody from Tommy and then I would go home and take a week or whatever, to really work on it. I like that much better. You know, when somebody's playing the piano, he may go off to another part of the song, to the bridge or something, and I'd still be stuck on the verse. And it's very hard for someone to play the same four bars over and over till I get it. This way I have the chance to think about what I want to write, to get the feeling of it.

"So I generally sit with a song about two or three days, playing it over and over, listening to it while I'm making the bed, or cleaning up. And then, generally, after about two or three days I get a feeling for it and the song just comes in about three-quarters of an hour, and I'll write the entire thing. Then I'll leave it alone that day and come back to it the next day to polish it and maybe try and change words, to make the meaning trickier.

"Generally I start from the top, first line, first verse, and go all the way through the song. I can't go to another line unless I have the line before it completed. A lot of people write lyrics and there's a line in there that's a really great, heavy line, but you say 'What the hell are they talking about?' because it has nothing to do with what they said before. To me, if you're going to state something, state it so that it's understandable. I believe in proper English, in completed thoughts, completed sentences.

"I write pretty basic lyrics, really basic emotions that would be very easy for anyone to identify with, but at the same time there's a certain depth to them. I don't write poems anymore— lyrics have taken up the need for writing poems. A couple of times I've written things on the spur of the moment—I'll get a surge and I might write out three pages of ideas and I'll keep them around and maybe pull a line from it or an idea that's really good. But basically, I know where everything comes from. I can identify everything because I only write from my own experience. The only song I didn't write from my own experience was 'Ghetto Child,' which is probably why I've always hated it."

I asked Linda who her major critic is.

"My husband. He's very good, excellent in fact. His most severe criticism would be 'I don't understand it. What does that mean?' I know if he doesn't understand a lyric, nobody else is going to understand it. He's not really a critic, but I generally get a feeling by watching his face exactly how it's hitting him. If it hits him right, then it's going to hit other people right."

How does Tommy Bell react to her lyrics?

"Tommy does not know anything about lyrics. I can say 'Mary had a little lamb,' if the syncopations are right, if the syllables fall gracefully with the music, he loves it. He may say something doesn't fit, but it's not because he doesn't like what it's saying. It would be that he doesn't like the sound of it. I really have to edit myself."

Does Linda ever comment on Tommy's melodies?

"If Tommy plays a melody for me and I don't like it, he throws it in the can. His philosophy has become, if I can't write a lyric to it, then something is wrong with the melody, so therefore, forget about it. Ninety-five percent of the time his melodies knock me out. If I don't like the meloly I can sit with it for weeks and nothing happens, nothing I say knocks me out, nothing means anything. 'Ghetto Child' took me forever to do because I didn't like the melody."

I wondered what the formative experiences were that led this white, Jewish girl into the world of rhythm and blues.

"Up until the age of fourteen I only knew about WIBG here in Philadelphia, which played 'Lipstick On Your Collar,' and stuff like that. I listened to it, but it didn't really kill me. Then one day I was watching the 'Ed Sullivan Show'—and I saw a guy named Smokey Robinson and the Miracles, who I'd never heard of, and he was singing 'You Really Got A Hold On Me,' and I was prostrated on the floor. That's music! There was something about it that just captured me.

"At that point I was just going into high school, and the school I went to was predominantly black. And over there they were listening to WDAS and WHAT, Georgie Woods and Jimmy Bishop. Where I lived I had trouble getting those stations, but I would listen through the static for hours. Then I sent away—you could get fourteen oldie records for a dollar. So I started catching up on all the things I had missed, the Cadillacs and all that, back to the beginning.

"Then it branched off into jazz. I started getting into jazz and going to the jazz festivals and so forth.

"Everybody laughed at me. My friends didn't quite understand. I mean, they would like a song, but I got into the *bass line!* From the moment I got into music, and particularly R 'n' B, people laughed. I became very black-oriented, because to know something you have to experience everything and only through feeling that experience can you know what you're talking about. So I was scorned all the way through.

"But Smokey's lyrics were spellbinding. I loved them. He said things simply, but it carried over into your emotions. I think if there's anybody I've taken my style of songwriting from, possibly my style has derived from Smokey."

Rhythm and Blues, although Linda's first love, is not her only musical pleasure.

"Crosby, Stills, Nash and Young send me right up the wall. Joni Mitchell is the queen. Her lyrics are excellent."

That same adjective has been applied to the lyrics of Linda Creed on more than one occasion in the pages of the better music journals and reviews.

"It makes me feel good when a deejay will say listen to the lyrics on this one, or something in a magazine says they're incredible, but it doesn't impress me. It makes me want to do better. I can definitely see my growth pattern, from say my first six songs, which were written over a number of years—I didn't write that much in the beginning because Tommy was doing a lot of outside production. My lyrics have gone from sad to happy, they're a bit more complicated, a bit wiser. The more of myself I've discovered, the more is in the songs. The early songs, like 'Free Girl,' 'Help Me Find A Way To Say I Love You,' were very corny. Even though I still write love songs I think they have much more depth than they did at that point, only because I had never experienced love. I didn't know what I was talking about.

"I've written some pretty strange lyrics for the Stylistics, 'Only For The Children.' 'A Baby's Born' for Johnny Mathis . . . about people dying and a baby being born. There have been quite a few where people have said 'Huh? R 'n' B? What are you getting at?' 'You Make Me Feel Brand New' is different from what people think of in the context of an R 'n' B tune. I don't think that we write R 'n' B, but that's beside the point."

Linda explained the curious reason behind her sudden lyric growth.

"Actually my lyric writing changed completely when I got married. For some reason it made me very creative. I guess it's because my husband inspires me. When I got married I had my first million seller, which I had written while we were engaged. 'You Make Me Feel Brand New,' is the biggest song we've had, and I was so happy while I was writing that song, each line I was jumping up and down saying 'I love it!'

"I'm basically a happy person, but before I got married I was writing sad tunes."

In the months to come Linda will finally achieve an all-but-forgotten dream.

"Presently I'm working on my own material, the music and the lyrics, for a solo album. It's a strange feeling, because usually I just have to worry about the lyrics, what they're going to say and how they'll feel; now I have to worry about things like chord structure. But the funny thing is, even now that I'm playing piano (badly) I don't say, here's a lyric I'll find chords to go with it. I play the chord and I feel what's going to come out of it. I get my content basically from the music. I never plan the song beforehand.

"I've got it so pat with lyric writing and really that's sad, even though I love what I do and I love writing. But I'm the kind of person who constantly wants a new challenge and since lyric writing has become kind of easy, the challenge doesn't exist, so now I have to go on to something else to challenge me—my own album. Once I accomplish that . . . who knows what I'll do. Of course, I'd love to do a show."

Although she'd originally intended to be a singer, this album won't necessarily launch her on a new career.

"I will not perform. I will never perform. I would just like to do the album for my own self-satisfaction. I work with performers every day and I see what happens to them. It's a very rough life. I was on the road, performing, when I tried to make it. Now I'm very happy at home. I'd like to be a mother someday. I want to have an equal balance between my business and my home life.

"Tommy and I have turned down several TV shows because he takes the bus to work every morning and he says 'How can I take the bus to work if people know who I am? They'll never leave me alone. How can I go into Pantry Pride and go shopping?' So I think that your personal life is too important. When you become a 'star' you tend to lose that."

I asked her if she wasn't already something of a "star," and what kind of problems that presents.

"The way it's evidenced is I don't know who really likes me for me, or just likes what I do. It's made me very selective as far as personal relationships are concerned, because I've had a number of bad experiences. My good friends are aware of everything I've done, but it's never discussed, it's never even brought up, which really makes me feel very good. When I had my first million seller they were all very happy for me, but that was it. It was like being Bar Mitzvahed or something."